INSTANT ENCYCLOPEDIA

Facts in a FLASH!

Published by Playmore Inc., Publishers, 58 Main Street, 2nd
Floor, Hackensack, N.J. 07601 and Waldman Publishing
Corp., 570 Seventh Avenue, New York, N.Y. 10018

Printed in Canada

bominable Snowman

The Abominable Snowman is also called the yeti. It is a huge, hairy, humanlike creature said to live on Mount Everest and other mountains in the Himalayas. Reports of the creature have also come from other parts of Asia, including Tibet and Nepal. Despite the claims of many people over the years, there is no solid proof that the Abominable Snowman exists.

Abominable Snowman

Alexander the Great

Alexander the Great (336–323 BC) was one of the greatest generals who ever lived. Before he reached the age of 33, he had conquered almost all of the world known in ancient times. He helped spread Greek culture from Asia Minor and Egypt to India.

alligator

Meat-eating reptile belonging to the same family as the crocodile. The male can grow up to twenty feet long and weigh 550 pounds. The female lays up to 80 eggs, which are about the size of a chicken's. The alligator is found in rivers and marshes from North Carolina to Florida.

An Abominable Word Challenge

How many words can you find hidden in the words "Abominable Snowman?" We found 19, but there are many more. Solution, see page 134.

Amazon River

South American river about 4,000 miles long, flowing from the Andes in Peru into northern Brazil and from there into the Atlantic Ocean.

Andes

Mountain system extending along the west coast of South America from Panama to Tierra del Fuego. Its highest peak is Mount Aconcagua (22,833 feet) in Argentina.

animation

A motion picture that is made from a series of drawings, or objects, that creates the appearance of movement. In traditional animation, a filmmaker photographs a drawing or an object for one frame of film only. Each time the image or object is photographed, it is slightly changed. Once the film is run through a projector, the pictures appear to move. Animation dates back to the 1800s. American movie studios began producing cartoons such as *Felix the Cat* and *Popeye*, in the early 1900s. Today, computers are used to make animated movies, such as *Toy Story*, *Shrek*, and *The Incredibles*.

ant

Black, brown, or red insect. It lives in colonies that are organized into workers, males, and a queen.

ant

There are many types of ants. Army ants travel in

4

long, narrow columns in search of prey. Some of these columns contain up to 20 million ants. Leaf-cutter ants grow a fungus and tend it like farmers.

Antarctica

Land surrounding the South Pole, completely covered by a 5,500,000-square-mile ice shelf. Antarctica is the fifth largest of Earth's seven continents. It is larger in area than Europe. It is the coldest, highest, windiest, and most southerly and remote continent.

APE

Highly intelligent animal that most closely resembles man. Apes include the chimpanzee, gorilla, orangutan, and gibbon. Unlike monkeys, apes are tailless, and their arms are usually longer than their legs.

FAST FACT

Walt Disney's *Steamboat Willie*, made in 1928, featured the debut of Mickey Mouse.

· ·

APISH ANAGRAMS

Unscramble these words and phrases to capture some primates. Solution, see page 134.

1. zap nice hem _____
2. big nob _____
3. log liar _____
4. a gun or ant _____
5. my keno _____

BARNUM, P.T.

Phineas Taylor Barnum (1810–1891). Showman and circus operator famous for "The Greatest Show on Earth," with sensational sideshows. In 1882, Barnum brought over Jumbo the elephant from England's London Zoo.

barracuda

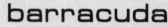

A large savage fish found in tropical waters. It has a long, slender, muscular body, large, saw-like teeth, protruding lower jaw, and yellowish green eyes. The great barracuda reaches eight feet in length. Swimmers have been attacked by them.

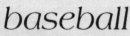

barracuda

baseball

A game played on a large field between two teams of 9 or 10 players on each team. The teams take turns playing offense, or batting, and playing defense, or fielding. The goal of the game is to score as many runs against the other team as possible by advancing around the four bases on the field and ending up back at home plate. Baseball began in the mid-1800s in the eastern part of the Untied States. The National League was founded in 1876, and the American League was founded in 1900.

bat

The only mammal that can fly. Bats have hands and arms modified to serve as wings. Nearly all bats are active at night. They use a form of sonar to navigate and find prey. This sonar also lets them steer clear of people. Bats are very useful. They eat tons of insect pests and pollinate 500 different kinds of plants, including bananas and figs.

bear

Large mammals with powerful limbs, shaggy fur, and a very short tail. Bears are generally peaceful if not bothered. Bears live in mountain and forest regions and Arctic wilderness. They are closely related to the dog and the raccoon. They include grizzlies, black bears, and the giant panda.

FAST FACT

> Baseball's world championship contest, the World Series, has been played every year since 1903, except for 1904 and 1994.

Get Your Bearings
bear in mind

1. gr_zzly
2. pol_r
3. pan_a
4. ho_ey

5. _lack
6. brui_
7. _alay
8. h_bernat_

Complete the words by filling in the missing letters with letters from the words on top. Use each letter in the words on top only once. Solution, see page 134.

beavers

Large rodents with soft, brown fur, chisel-like teeth, webbed hind feet, and a flat, broad tail. They gnaw down trees, and build dams to form beaver ponds. There they build dry island lodges with underwater entrances.

bees

Industrious, broad-bodied, four-winged, hairy insects with biting and sucking mouth parts. Bees gather pollen and nectar, and make and store honey.

Beethoven, Ludwig van

Ludwig van Beethoven (1770–1827) is often called the greatest composer of all time. He wrote symphonies, piano concertos, piano sonatas, and string quartets. One of his most well known pieces is his Ninth Symphony.

beetle

Beetles represent more than one-third of all known insect species. Some scientists believe there could be more than 350,000 species of beetles worldwide. Some beetles are only about 0.01 inch long, but the harmless rhinoceros beetles may be three inches long. The African goliath beetle weighs almost three ounces, more than many birds.

BLACK WIDOW SPIDER

The black widow is the most poisonous spider in the United States. The female was thought to eat its mate,

but this is not true.
Its black body
has a red mark
underneath
shaped like an
hourglass. Only
the female black
widow spider is
dangerous to
people.

black widow spider

FAST FACT

The smallest beetle in the world is the feather-winged beetle. It is smaller than the period at the end of this sentence.

Scrambled Bees

Unscramble the letters to find words about bees.

Solution, see page 134.

1. onhye   _ _ _ _ _
2. gsitn   _ _ _ _ _
3. ueqne   _ _ _ _ _
4. iehv   _ _ _ _
5. lebmub   _ _ _ _ _ _

C actus

Prickly plants well adapted for life in dry climates. They have fleshy stems and branches with spines and beautiful flowers. Some varieties are popular as house plants because they require little care and have interesting shapes.

Caesar, Julius

Julius Caesar (c. 100–44 BC) was a Roman general and ruler who built the greatest of all ancient empires. He made Rome the center of an empire that spread across Europe. His political enemies feared his power so much that they banded together to kill him. William Shakespeare, the English playwright, wrote a play about Caesar's life and death, *Julius Caesar*. It is believed that he wrote it around 1599.

camel

Large, strange looking, cud-chewing mammal with one or two humps on its back. The humps store fat, not water. The camel is used to carry people and heavy loads in the desert. It can go for a long time without food or water. Camels can close their nostrils to keep out dirt and sand.

Camp David

Presidential retreat in northern Maryland. Originally called Shangri-La by President Franklin D. Roosevelt. Renamed Camp David by President Dwight D. Eisenhower for his grandson.

canyon

A deep, narrow valley or gorge between high cliffs. A canyon is created by a river eating away the rock around it. Some canyons are huge. The Grand Canyon of the Colorado River is 278 miles long and more than 5,000 feet deep. The Fish River Canyon in Namibia, Africa, is 100 miles long and almost 1,600 feet deep in some places.

FAST FACT

The red blood cells of camels are oval, instead of circular, as in all other mammals.

Camel Confusion

These three camels look very similar, but only two are exactly alike. Can you find the camel that's different? Solution, see page 134.

#1

#2

#3

caribou

A large deer, also called reindeer. It lives in the Arctic tundra, forests, and mountainous regions. Many caribou migrate in huge herds every year — sometimes as far as 2,000 miles. Unlike any other species of deer, female caribou grow antlers. Male caribou can grow antlers more than four feet long.

Carver, George Washington

George Washington Carver (c. 1860–1943) was an African American scientist who worked with plants. He developed more than 300 products from plants. His best-known work was with peanuts, sweet potatoes, soybeans, and cotton.

CASTLE

The castle was the stronghold of a European king or nobleman in the Middle Ages. It was a large, fortified building or group of buildings, with thick walls and a moat. The moat was a wide, deep ditch usually filled with water. The only entrance into the castle was by way of a drawbridge. The drawbridge, which was raised every night, stretched across the moat.

cat, domestic

This small, agile, soft-furred mammal has been kept since ancient times as a pet and for killing rats and mice. It can draw its claws back and in. There are almost 40 varieties, or breeds, of domestic cats. An estimated 30 million domestic or house cats share our homes.

FAST FACT

George Washington Carver created a
milk substitute from peanuts.

Castle Maze

Help the knight make his way through the castle to rescue the
fair maiden. Solution, see page 135.

CAVE

Hollow place beneath the earth, or in the side of a hill or mountain. Many caves have openings to the surface. There are almost 6,000 caves in the United States. The longest cave in the world is Mammoth Cave, Kentucky, a National Park. It is almost 350 miles long. Prehistoric humans who lived in caves are called cave dwellers.

CHEETAH

A long-legged member of the cat family that is about the size of a leopard. It is one of the fastest-moving of all animals. It can reach a top speed of 60 miles per hour in 2 seconds, and maintain it for 1,000 feet. The cheetah hunts the fastest animals: zebra, antelope, and wildebeest.

comic books

Books that contain a story, or stories, told through words and sequential pictures. The first American comic books were published in the mid-1930s. They mostly reprinted comic strips originally printed in newspapers. These comic books proved to be very popular. The first superhero comic book was published in 1938. *Action Comics* featured the debut of *Superman*. Soon there were dozens of superhero comic books such as *Batman*, *Wonder Woman*, and years later, *The Amazing Spider-Man*, *X-Men*, and *The Incredible Hulk*. Today, hundreds of comic books are published every month, with subjects ranging from superhero stories to action, science fiction, mystery, horror, and even nonfiction.

Crypto-Cartoon

To translate from the cave-dweller language, decode the caption by using the handy decoder. Solution, see page 135.

x y z a b c d e f g h i j k l m n o p q r s t u v w
a b c d e f g h i j k l m n o p q r s t u v w x y z

"F qefkh fq'p qfjb tb jlsba fkql qeb mbkqelrpb."

15

d am

Dams block the flow of a waterway. Dams and the reservoirs behind them help control floods. Many dams use the energy of falling water to generate electric power. Dams also hold water for drinking and crop irrigation.

desert

A desert is a parched region that is empty of most living things. A desert receives less than 10 inches of rain in a year. Daytime temperatures can reach 130° Fahrenheit in the shade. At night, the temperature can drop to near freezing. When rains do come to the desert, the soil, unprotected by plants, easily erodes.

dinosaur

An extinct reptile-like creature that ruled the earth for more than 140 million years. Its name was coined by Richard Owen, a British scientist, in 1842. "Dinosaur" means "terrible lizard."

Dinosaurs did not look much like the land animals of today. Some dinosaurs walked upright like today's birds and many mammals, but some walked on all fours like crocodiles and lizards. The giant Aparosaurus was 80 feet long, while the little Compsognathus was about the same size as a chicken.

FAST FACT

Many scientists believe that birds are the descendants of dinosaurs.

Aparosaurus

Build Your Own Dinosaur

When dinosaur scientists discover a new dinosaur, they give it a name from Greek or Latin that tries to describe it. To name some newly discovered dinosaurs, take a word from column A and match it to a phrase in column B. Then, add the word from column B to the word "saurus or "saur," meaning "lizard," to get a new dinosaur name. The first one has been done for you. Solution, see page 135.

Column A	Column B	Column C
Hydro = water	1. A yellow-colored monster	1. Xanthosaur
Ophi = snake	2. Lots of teeth	2. _____
Xantho = yellow	3. Narrow body	3. _____
Sagitta = narrow	4. More like a snake	4. _____
Dent = teeth	5. Likes the water	5. _____

17

dirigible

Unlike airplanes or heli-
copters, which are
heavier than
air, a slow-
moving dirigible
is lighter than
air. It is filled
with a gas
that lifts it off
the ground. It's like a hot-air bal-
loon that can be steered and driven. Dirigibles are
sometimes called blimps or zeppelins.

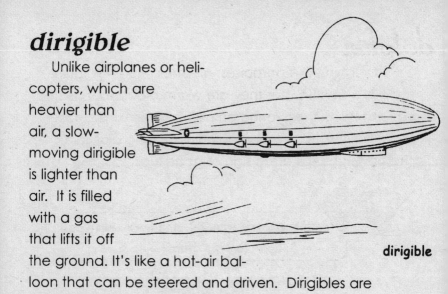

dirigible

Disney, Walt

Walt Disney (1901–1966) created animated cartoons
featuring characters such as Mickey Mouse and
Donald Duck. He produced such animated films as
Snow White and the Seven Dwarfs (1937), *Pinocchio*
(1940), and *Fantasia* (1940). He also built Disneyland
amusement parks that are visited by several million
people every year.

dog

The dog is related to the common wolf. It is also a
cousin of the fox, jackal, and coyote. There are almost 300
dog breeds. The dog is a beloved companion that serves
people in many ways. It is used for hunting, for police
work, and as a service animal for the disabled.

dolphin

Dolphins, like porpoises, are mammals. Dolphins may look like fish, but they are warm-blooded, breathe air, and nurse their young on milk, just like other mammals. Sailors believe that dolphins cruising alongside the bows of ships are a sign of good luck.

FAST FACT

Walt Disney won 29 Academy Awards for his films.

Quotable Canine

First fill in as many of the clues as you can. Then transfer the letters you have written into the quotation box. You'll see words beginning to form. Then work back and forth between the clues and the quotation box. To start you off, we have filled in number 18. Hint: The quotation is one about dogs by Bernard of Clairvaux, a dog-lover of long ago. Solution see page 135.

1	2	3		4	5	6	7	8		9	10		11	12	13	14
			15	16	17	18 O		19	20	21	22		23	24		
25	26	27														

weighs a lot
$\overline{2}\ \overline{7}\ \overline{15}\ \overline{6}\ \overline{24}$

cow calls
$\overline{23}\ \overline{20}\ \overline{3}\ \overline{17}$

A, E, I, O, or U
$\overline{21}\ \overline{5}\ \overline{11}\ \overline{22}\ \overline{16}$

not tame
$\overline{1}\ \overline{12}\ \overline{4}\ \overline{25}$

sadness
$\overline{27}\ \overline{19}\ \overline{26}\ \overline{5}\ \overline{9}$

market
$\overline{8}\ \overline{10}\ \overline{13}\ \overline{14}$

Earth

Earth is the third planet from the sun. It is the planet on which humans live. Earth is the only planet known to have life on it. About 71 percent of Earth's surface is covered by water, which is needed for life as we know it to exist. The rest is land, mostly in the form of continents.

Edison, Thomas Alva

Thomas Alva Edison (1847–1931) patented more than 1,000 inventions. He invented the electric lightbulb, the motion picture projector, the telephone transmitter, an improved battery, and even a voting machine.

Egypt, ancient

This mighty civilization along the Nile River in northeastern Africa lasted for more than 3,000 years. No other country has such a long, unbroken history as Egypt. Though it looks strange, the writing (hieroglyphics) of ancient Egypt can be read by scholars. It tells us much about this interesting civilization. The ancient Egyptians built great stone temples and pyramids, and their ships traded with many lands.

FAST FACT

The tusks of elephants continue to grow throughout the elephant's life.

elephant

There are two kinds of elephants. Asian elephants live in India, China, and Southeast Asia. African elephants live in Africa south of the Sahara. Asian elephants are smaller than African elephants. African elephants weigh up to 15,000 pounds and stand about 13 feet high. Asian elephants weigh up to 11,000 pounds and stand about 10 feet high. Elephants live on leaves, grass, fruit, bark, and roots. They eat as much as 660 pounds of food, and drink more than 50 gallons of water every day.

Pair of Pyramids

These four pyramids look somewhat similar, but only two are exactly alike. Can you find the two that match? Solution, see page 135.

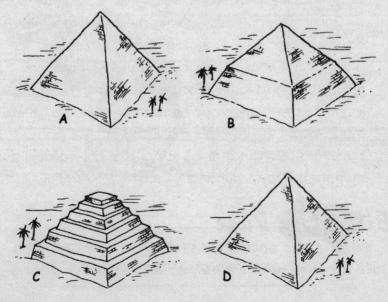

elevator

Carries people and materials from one floor to another. Elisha Otis invented the elevator in 1852, His invention meant that people no longer had to climb a lot of stairs to reach the tops of tall buildings. The elevator made possible very high skyscrapers such as the Empire State Building in New York City and the Sears Tower in Chicago.

Elizabeth I, Queen

Elizabeth I (1533–1603) was queen of England during a time of great achievement and prosperity. She was called Good Queen Bess and was very popular.

elk

A member of the deer family. An adult male is called a stag and weighs up to 750 pounds. Its antlers can each reach more than four feet long.

elk

Ellington, Duke

Edward Kennedy Ellington (1899–1974) was known as Duke Ellington. He was a very popular pianist and band leader. He was an important pioneer in big-band jazz. He composed more than 1,500 songs.

elm

The beautiful elm tree can reach a height of 120 feet. The inner bark of the slippery elm was once used as a thirst quencher. Because of its sweet taste, it was also chewed.

FAST FACT

Duke Ellington began playing piano at the age of seven. He made his debut as a professional musician at the age of seventeen.

EL Quiz

How many of these "EL" words can you name?
Put one letter on each blank. Solution, see page 136.

1. Santa's little helper   E L _
2. Tree   E L _
3. Member of deer family   E L _
4. Part of arm   E L _ _ _
5. Lifts people up   E L _ _ _ _ _ _
6. English queen   E L _ _ _ _ _ _ _
7. Jazz duke   E L _ _ _ _ _ _ _
8. Trunk-and-tusks beast   E L _ _ _ _ _ _
9. Subatomic particle   E L _ _ _ _ _ _
10. Type of eel   E L _ _ _ _ _ _

emerald

A bright green emerald is one of the most valued of gemstones. A perfect emerald is more expensive than a diamond of the same weight. The costliest emeralds come from Colombia.

emu

The emu is a big bird that cannot fly. Second largest of all birds, the emu of Australia is more than six feet tall. The feathers of an emu look like rough hair. The feathers are special because they help the Emu deal with extreme weather changes.

emu

English language

The most widespread language on Earth is English. English is the national language of many countries, including the United States, Great Britain, Australia, and New Zealand. The English vocabulary is larger than that of any other language in the world.

equator

The equator is the imaginary east-west line that circles Earth midway between the North and South Poles. It divides our planet into the Northern and Southern Hemispheres.

escalator

Escalators are stairways moving from one floor of a building to the next. Escalators are found mostly in large stores and busy public buildings such as airports. The first escalator was installed in a department store in Philadelphia, Pennsylvania, in 1901.

....

Human Words

Many people have given their names to English words. These English words are called eponyms. Can you identify the eponyms from the following clues? To start things off, we've given you the answer to number 1. Solution, see page 136.

1. **Bump in the front of the neck named for the first man.**
   Answer: _____ **Adam's apple** _____

2. **Turncoat, named for a Revolutionary War general who was a traitor.** _____

3. **Special raised print alphabet used by blind people, invented by a blind Frenchman.** _____

4. **Luxury car, named for the founder of Detroit.** _____

5. **Mystery writers' award, named for the inventor of the detective story.** _____

6. **Signature, named for the first signer of the Declaration of Independence.** _____

7. **The capital of Liberia, named for the fifth president of the United States.** _____

Europe

Europe is about 3,998,000 square miles in size, or 7 percent of the world's land area. It has a population of more than 725,000,000. It consists of 47 independent countries.

explorers

Explorers travel to distant places and strange lands. They make long and difficult journeys for many reasons. In the past, they were looking for new trade routes and markets or to claim new lands for their kings. Others were looking for fame and fortune. Today, explorers are scientists investigating the most remote places on Earth, in the deepest parts of the ocean, and in space.

eyeglasses

Eyeglasses are made of glass or hard plastic, and are used to help correct people's vision by helping them see small things better, to see printed words clearer, or to see

farther. We even have special eyeglasses or goggles that protect workers' eyes from harm. Sunglasses are eyeglasses that are colored or tinted to help protect eyes against harmful rays of the sun.

Benjamin Franklin wearing bifocals

In 1784, Benjamin Franklin invented special eyeglasses called bifocals.

What Did He Find?

Can you identify the explorers' discoveries from the clues we've given? Solution, see page 136.

Example: This river has six letters. It starts with H and ends with N, and it was named for an explorer whose first name was Henry. Answer: Hudson

1. The name of this strait has six letters. It starts with B and ends with G, and separates Asia (Russia) from North America (Alaska), and was named for a Danish explorer.

2. The name of this state has seven letters. It starts with F and ends with A. It was discovered in 1513 by Spanish explorer Juan Ponce de León.

3. The name of this very cold island has nine letters. It starts with G and ends with D, and was discovered by a Viking.

4. The name of this ocean has seven letters. It starts with P and ends with C, and was named by Spanish explorer Vasco Núñez de Balboa.

5. The name of this country has six letters. It starts with M and ends with O, and was conquered by Spanish conquistador Hernán Cortés.

*f*alcon

The falcon is the most skillful bird of prey. Other birds of prey include the buzzard, condor, eagle, osprey, and owl. The falcon feeds on small birds and rodents. When hunting, the falcon rises above and dives down on its prey. The falcon looks like a streamlined hawk with long pointed wings, and ranges in size from about 8 to 24 inches long. Some falcons live in cities, making their nests on tall buildings.

FAST FACT

In archery, feathers are still used to help arrows fly straight.

feather

Only birds grow feathers. Feathers protect the bird against water and cold, and help the bird fly. Feathers are mostly made from a substance called beta keratin. Because of their beauty, we once used feathers to decorate clothing and hats. This led to the killing of many birds to get their feathers. Now birds are protected. Before the invention of fountain pens and ballpoint pens, the hollow part of the feather, the quill, was used as a writing tool.

fern

Ferns are green plants that have been around for millions of years. At one time, the planet was covered by fern forests. Ferns do not have flowers or seeds. Instead, they reproduce by spores. Ferns like to grow in damp places.

Their leaves are called fronds, and are green and feathery. Early in spring, the fronds begin to uncurl and look like the necks of violins, and are so called fiddleheads.

falcon

•••

Spot the Birds of Prey

Ronald and Buddy like to spot birds. They keep a record of their finds in code. The code is made up by using the names of six birds of prey. The names have been scrambled. Can you figure out what six birds are hidden below? Solution, see page 136.

Ron: "Bud, razz a low glee, per soy cod on calf."

1. _____   4. _____

2. _____   5. _____

3. _____   6. _____

fingerprint

It was in the 1890s that police began using fingerprints to identify criminals. A fingerprint is an impression of the tiny ridge patterns on the fingertip. It is used for identification. No two persons have exactly the same arrangement of these lines, and the lines remain the same throughout a person's life. Fingerprints are filed according to the ridge patterns.

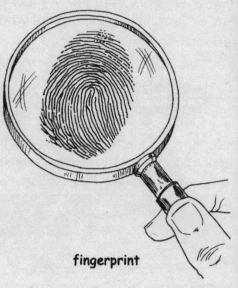

fingerprint

fireplace

The fireplace was one of the earliest ways to heat a home. The first fireplaces were nothing more than pits in the middle of the house. They had to serve as stoves, sources of light, and protection against wild animals. Nowadays, fireplaces are just cozy stone hearths with a chimney. They may not work as well as more modern heat sources, but they are snug and attractive.

fish

A fish is a cold-blooded animal with a backbone that lives in water. It breathes with the help of gills. It normally has several sets of fins, and most fish are covered with scales. More than 25,000 kinds of fish are now known, with new fish being discovered at the rate of 250 species a year. Fish range from the tiny little goby, which is less than half an inch long, to the giant whale shark, which can reach 40 feet in length.

FAST FACT

The Federal Bureau of Investigation (FBI) in Washington, D.C., has the world's largest fingerprint collection — more than 235 million fingerprint cards.

Change a Letter to Catch a Fish

Sometimes a word can be changed into the name of a fish just by changing one of its letters. Example: Change one letter in a musical instrument to make a fish. Answer: Harp > Carp.

Catch a fish by changing just one letter in each of the following words. Solution, see page 136.

1. Change one letter in a fishing pole to make a fish. _____

2. Change one letter in a journey to make a fish. _____

3. Change one letter in a hut to make a fish. _____

4. Change one letter in a cavity to make a fish. _____

5. Change one letter in a melody to make a fish. _____

6. Change one letter in a baby dog to make a fish. _____

7. Change one letter in a fruit to make a fish. _____

8. Change one letter in an electric arc to make a fish. _____

9. Change one letter in an election lineup to make a fish. _____

flag

A piece of cloth that is used as an emblem, a symbol of a country, or as a signal. Flags are also called banners, standards, pennants, or ensigns, depending on how they are used. The Egyptians and Chinese were the first peoples to use flags.

FLAMINGO

A large water bird with very long legs and neck. It's often taller than six feet. Its feathers are usually rosy pink. The beautiful flamingo flies in large flocks with its neck and legs outstretched. The flamingo feeds mostly on mollusks, such as clams. When eating, a flamingo dips its head under water and scoops backward with its head upside down. Flamingos live in many parts of the world, including Africa and southern Asia.

forest

A thick growth of trees and other woody plants covering a large piece of land. The first community (town) forest was established in Newington, New Hampshire in 1710. The first national forest reserve was the Yellowstone Park Timber Stands Reserve (now Shoshone National Forest) in Wyoming, established in 1891. Almost 200 million acres, or more than one-fourth of the entire forest area of the United States, is taken care of by the U.S. Forest Service.

FAST FACT

The fox is a very fast runner and can easily reach a speed of 30 miles per hour.

fox

The fox is the smallest member of the canine family. Foxes eat rats, rabbits, and even large insects. Because their prey is small, foxes don't need the help of other foxes in hunting. That's why foxes live alone, instead of in packs. The red fox, the most common species, weighs about 15 pounds and is about 40 inches long with a tail that's another 15 inches in length.

fox

Design Your Own Flag

Here's a chance to create your very own flag.

Galahad, Sir

The only knight of the Round Table who had pure virtue. Sir Galahad succeeded in his quest for the Holy Grail, when King Arthur's other knights failed.

GALAXY

Galaxies are huge groups of stars. A large galaxy may contain as many as a trillion stars. The sun, Earth, and all the other planets of the solar system are in a galaxy called the Milky Way. All the stars you can see at night without a telescope are in the Milky Way.

FAST FACT

Astronomers estimate that there are more than 120 billion galaxies in the universe.

galley

A galley is a long, narrow ship that was commonly used during ancient times. These ships used oars and sails to propel them across the water. Many gallies were more than 100 feet long. Slaves, prisoners of war, and convicts were used to row the oars of the galley.

gazelle

The gazelle is a graceful, lightly built, and gentle member of the antelope family found in Asia and Africa. Gazelles are fast runners that can instantly change the direction in which they are running. In one variety called Grant's gazelle, the horns can extend almost two and a half feet in length.

gazelle

....

Galaxy Grouping

Read the list below and circle the galaxies that are real.
Solution, see page 136.

1.   **The Andromeda Galaxy**

2.   **The Hercules Galaxy**

3.   **The Oceanic Galaxy**

4.   **The Milky Way Galaxy**

35

gecko

The gecko is a small and harmless lizard that lives on insects. Geckos can be spotted at night in the tropics running upside down on the ceilings of houses. They can cling to smooth surfaces, such as ceilings and the sides of buildings, because they have adhesive disks on their toes. Although they are not native to the United States, they are now found in the south, having stowed away on ships from Asian countries. They are sometimes kept as pets because they will feed on household pests such as cockroaches.

gecko

FAST FACT

Unlike other lizards, geckos make a chirping or clicking sound, instead of a hiss.

gemstone

Gemstones are rare and valuable minerals that can be turned into beautiful jewels. They include diamonds, rubies, emeralds, opals, and sapphires.

Gemstone Fill-ins

Write a different letter of the alphabet onto each of the blank spaces below to form the name of a gemstone. Each gemstone has five or more letters reading across. You can put the letter at the beginning of the word, the middle, or at the tail end. Use each letter only once. When you use a letter, cross it off in the list. Remember, not every letter in a row is always used to form the word. We've started off the puzzle with the answer to number 1. Solution, see page 136.

Letter List:

A B C D E F G H I J K L M N O P Q R S T U V W X Y Z

1. Z E M E R <u>A</u> L D K C X
2. W T D I A __ O N D L O
3. T S A P P __ I R E C F
4. P B D K O __ A L G N Q
5. U C E R U __ Y M F B S
6. A M E T H __ S T R V Y

Geronimo

Geronimo (1829–1909) was the leader of the Chiricahua Apache tribe in the southwestern United States. For many years, he fought against being removed from his tribal lands. His bravery and military skills won him respect from everyone. Finally, his small band of warriors had to surrender to the U.S. government.

Geronimo

GEYSER

Hot spring that throws forth jets of hot water and steam, sometimes at regular intervals. The eruption can be as high as 325 feet. Old Faithful at Yellowstone National Park is a geyser. It expels almost 12,000 gallons of water in a 165-foot-high column every time it erupts.

giraffe

The tallest of living animals, the giraffe grows up to an amazing 17 feet. Its body is smaller than that of a horse, though. All its height comes from its very long legs and five-foot-long neck.

 FAST FACT

When the gentle giraffe kicks out with its long and strong legs, even ferocious lions will retreat.

Miser Geyser

"Miser geyser" is a pair of rhyming words. What are the pairs that fit the following clues? Solution, see page 137.

(Example: A cheap, hot spring = Miser Geyser)

1. Old Faithful consultant?

2. Hot pepper enjoyed by Plains tribe?

3. Little Big Horn general's group?

4. Tall animal's water pitcher?

glacier

A glacier is a body of ice, snow, water, and rock that slowly moves down a slope or valley, or flows outward on a land surface. Ten percent of Earth's land area is covered by glaciers. Ice sheets and glaciers make up more than 75 percent of all the fresh water on our planet. If all the ice melted, the oceans would rise by 200 feet.

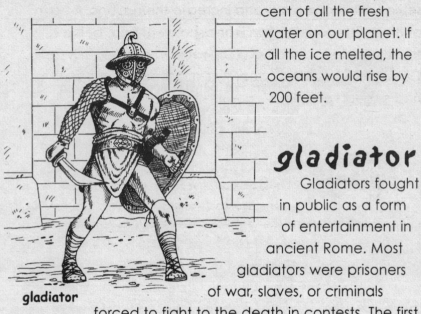

gladiator

gladiator

Gladiators fought in public as a form of entertainment in ancient Rome. Most gladiators were prisoners of war, slaves, or criminals forced to fight to the death in contests. The first gladiator games were held around 264 BC.

gnu

A large African antelope that looks like a buffalo. It has a head like an ox, a tail like a horse, and a heavy face and shoulders. Its horns curve downward and outward.

Although gnus look threatening, they are actually playful animals. When humans come near, the gnus will jump around, run off, and then stop suddenly to look back to see if they're being followed.

gold rush

In 1848, gold was discovered in a quiet part of northern California. In 1849, the gold rush was in full swing with large groups of prospectors coming to California. These prospectors were called the forty-niners. They helped settle unknown regions and increase the national wealth of the entire country. San Francisco went from being a small town to a city of 25,000 people in one year. By 1850, California was able to apply for statehood because it had enough people living there to do so.

FAST FACT — The ice cap covering Antarctica is the world's largest glacier.

Return the Gold

Parts of each of the following "gold" items have been removed. Put back the removed part to fill out the "gold" item. Solution, see page 137.

| Whoopi | ager | oldie | retriever |

1. Movie and TV actress _____ Goldberg
2. Senior citizen   golden_____
3. Hit from the past   golden_____
4. Dog   golden_____

hailstones

Hailstones are balls of ice and snow that fall, often during a thunderstorm, in the spring and summer. Hailstones form when water freezes around an ice crystal. They can be as big as softballs, or larger, and may damage crops and property and injure livestock and people.

Hale, Nathan

Nathan Hale

Nathan Hale (1755–1776) was a hero of the American Revolution (1775–1783). He was captured on his way back from collecting information on British troop positions for General George Washington. British General William Howe ordered Hale to be hanged as a spy. Hale's last words were, "I only regret that I have but one life to lose for my country."

Hannibal

Hannibal (247–183 BC) was a brilliant general who almost defeated Rome using elephants like modern-day tanks. His country, Carthage, a Phoenician nation in

North Africa, was an enemy of Rome. His march on Rome from Spain across the Alps in 218 BC with 40,000 troops is one of the greatest military feats in history. His crossing of the Alps was celebrated with Carthaginian coins that showed Hannibal's face on one side and an elephant on the other.

hawk

Fast-flying birds of prey that hunt during the day rather than at night. They are armed with strong, hooked bills and long, very sharp claws, or talons. They have the sharpest vision of any animal. They eat other birds, squirrels, mice, rabbits, frogs, and snakes.

Hailstone Words

How many words can you make from the word HAILSTONES? We found 12. Solution, see page 137.

1. _____
2. _____
3. _____
4. _____
5. _____
6. _____
7. _____
8. _____
9. _____
10. _____
11. _____
12. _____

heart

The heart is the center of the circulatory system. It pumps blood throughout the body at a rate of more than about 4 quarts per minute. The heart of an adult weighs between about 8 and 12 ounces, and beats an average of 72 times per minute. During a lifetime of 70 years, it will beat about 2.5 billion times and pump a total of 35 million gallons or more of blood.

FAST FACT

> The heart of an average person pumps about 2,000 gallons of blood in just one day.

helicopter

The helicopter is an aircraft that can hover in midair and fly forward, backward, or sideways. It can take off and land in a small area without needing a runway. It is also known as a chopper, whirlybird, or eggbeater. Besides its essential military work, the helicopter is used in civilian emergency medical services, search and rescue missions, police work, news and traffic reporting, and for commuter and business travel.

herbs

Plants used in cooking and medicine. In ancient Egypt, Greece, and Rome, they were used to make dull food taste better, and to treat different ailments. Today they are still used as seasonings to enhance the flavor of food. Herbs include basil, bay, chervil, marjoram, mint, oregano, parsley, rosemary, sage, savory, tarragon, thyme, licorice, caraway, and dill.

Hercules

Hercules was the son of Zeus, the king of the Greek gods. He was the strongest and most courageous hero of classical Greek mythology. Against all odds, he performed feats that everyone thought were impossible. In legend, he was the only mortal to be granted immortality.

Hercules

My Herb Garden

Unscramble the letters to find the herbs. Solution, see page 137.

1. ratgonra _____
2. idll _____
3. sega _____
4. hemyt _____
5. yab _____

HIEROGLYPHICS

The writing system of ancient Egypt dating back to 3000 BC. that used pictures. Hieroglyphics ("sacred carving") were used for prayers and other sacred purposes.

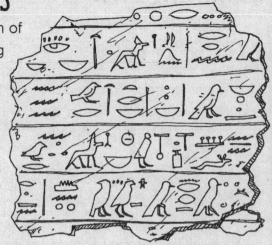

hieroglyphics

hippopotamus

The name hippopotamus means "river horse," though hippos are actually cousins of pigs. An adult hippopotamus may weigh 4 tons, grow to a length of 15 feet, and stand 5 feet tall at the shoulder. It is one of the largest and heaviest land animals, with huge jaws and tusks. The hippo is capable of biting through small boats and slicing crocodiles in two.

honey

A sweet, thick, and syrupy sugar solution, honey is produced by bees from plant nectar. Nectar is a kind of sweet sap. To produce about a pound of honey requires 25,000 trips between the hive and flowers. A pound of honey contains the essence of about 2 million flowers.

hummingbird

Because of their small size and constant activity, brightly colored hummingbirds must feed every 10 to 15 minutes. Hummingbirds feed on nectar at the rate of about 13 licks per second. An especially long tongue allows the hummingbird to reach nectar deep within a flower.

hyena

The hyena is incorrectly believed to be a cowardly scavenger that lives only on scraps and carrion. Actually, it is a fierce and fearless nocturnal hunter. Hyenas can run up to 40 miles per hour, and their packs can bring down zebras and other large animals.

FAST FACT

Hyenas sometimes travel in packs of up to 100.

. . . .

Sweet Words

nectar	1. _____
honey	2. _____
blossom	3. _____
hive	4. _____
bee	5. _____

Put the "honey" words in alphabetical order. Solution, see page 137.

Iceberg

A large floating mass of ice. Icebergs are the broken-off ends of glaciers that slide into the sea. They can be mountains of ice a mile or more across and more than 200 feet above the water. Icebergs can endanger shipping. The *Titanic* was sunk in 1912 by an iceberg.

ice cream

Popular frozen dairy food made of sugars, milk products, and flavorings. The Chinese probably invented ice cream around 2000 BC. It was first made in Italy in the 17th century. It came to the United States a few years later. George Washington purchased an ice-cream maker on May 17, 1784.

Iceland

An island republic in the North Atlantic, about 600 miles west of Norway. It was discovered by Norsemen about 870 AD. Iceland is only about 40,000 square miles in size, and has less than 300,000 people. Its official language is Icelandic, which is related to Norwegian, German, and English.

FAST FACT

Iceland has the world's oldest parliament, founded in 930 AD.

igloo

The igloo is a round, snow house built by the Inuit or Eskimo peoples of the far north. It holds in heat because snow is a good insulator. It also protects against the wind. A man can put up an igloo in an hour. During the summer months, when the igloos melt, the Inuits live in portable tents made of caribou or seal hides.

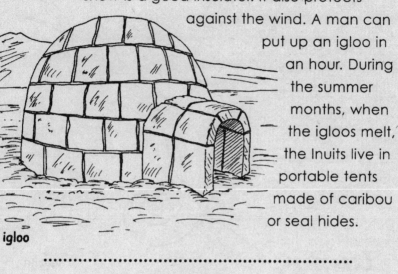

igloo

....

Ice Quiz

How many of these "ICE" words can you name? Put one letter on each blank. Solution, see page 137.

1. girl in Wonderland   _____ICE

2. cops   _____ICE

3. learner   _____ICE

4. selection   _____ICE

5. rehearse   _____ICE

49

iguana

Most of these large lizards are green. Many have saw-like teeth. The iguana of Central and South America can be 7 feet long and may weigh up to 30 pounds. It lives on leaves and other plants.

iguana

Incas

In the 1400s, the Incas ruled an empire that stretched 3,000 miles north and south through the Andes Mountains of South America. They occupied what is now Peru, and parts of Bolivia, Chile, Ecuador, and Argentina. They were master builders who could fit stones securely together without cement or mortar. The city of Cuzco, situated in southern Peru, was the Inca capital.

FAST FACT

"Internet" is short for "interconnected network of networks."

insect

A small, air-breathing invertebrate, or animal without backbone, with a body that has three main parts—head, thorax, and abdomen. Adult insects usually have three pairs of legs, one pair of antennae, and two pairs of wings.

About one million species of insects have been found so far, about half of all the animals known to science. They are found everywhere on Earth, but only a few live in the ocean. Insects range in size from the 0.01-inch dwarf beetle to the 20-inch-long walking stick of Southeast Asia.

Internet

The Internet is a large network of computers that connects businesses, institutions, and people all over the world. The Internet was started in the late 1960s by the United States Department of Defense. The department set up a network of military and university computers to share information.

Insect Inspection

Fill in the missing letter to complete each insect name. Solution, see page 137.

1. _ee
2. _eetle
3. a_t
4. ter_ite
5. mosq_ito

iron

Iron is the fourth most common element in Earth's crust. Next to aluminum, it is the most abundant of all metals. Both plants and animals contain very small amounts of iron. Iron was used for ornaments and weapons in prehistoric times. Some iron beads found in Egypt date back to 4,000 BC. Iron is the basic material in steel.

island

Any small body of land completely surrounded by water. The largest island in the world is Greenland, with an area of just under 850,000 square miles. The only island state in the United States is Hawaii.

ivory

Hard white material obtained from the tusks of elephants, hippopotamuses, whales, walruses, and narwhals. Ivory is a form of dental enamel. Blue-colored fossil ivory, from northern Siberia, is from the 16-foot-long tusks of mammoths, huge prehistoric elephants.

elephant

ivy

Climbing or creeping plants. They climb with sucker-like disks that attach themselves to walls or trees, or by means of climbing tendrils, or special stems or branches. Ivy helps keep walls dry and warm, and adds beauty. It rarely hurts the spots where it climbs, except when rootlets find their way into cracks in a wall.

FAST FACT

> Before the invention of plastics, ivory was used to make billiard balls and piano keys.

Island Discovery Challenge

How many islands can you find in this grid? You'll have to sail down, backwards, and forwards. Solution, see page 137.

```
Q  J  A  M  A  I  C  A  O  E  L  B  A

N  A  B  X  Z  U  W  D  Y  A  X  A  N

Q  V  M  I  L  A  B  X  H  P  W  X  O

M  A  L  T  A  V  C  U  B  A  K  D  I
```

jackal

Related to dogs and wolves, jackals are both scavengers and predators. They will hunt and kill birds, small mammals, and insects. They are about 3 feet long and weigh up to 24 pounds. They travel in pairs or packs, or sometimes alone. Their reputation for cowardice is undeserved. They are brave and intelligent animals.

jaguar

The only "big cat" in the Americas. It can reach 7 feet in length. It lives in swamps and forests. While an excellent swimmer, it hunts mainly on the ground or in trees. Its prey is mostly pig-like peccaries, capybaras (a giant rodent), fish, and even crocodiles.

James, Jesse

Jesse James (1847–1882) robbed banks, stagecoaches, and trains carrying gold from Arkansas to Colorado and Texas. He was killed by a fellow gang member for a reward of $10,000.

Jesse James

Jefferson, Thomas

Thomas Jefferson (1743–1826) was the third president of the United States. He wrote the Declaration of Independence and the Virginia Statute for Religious Freedom, and founded the University of Virginia. He acquired the Louisiana Purchase, a vast territory west of the Mississippi River, for $15 million in 1803. Jefferson commissioned the Lewis and Clark Expedition, which explored the central and northwestern territories of the United States from 1803 to 1806. Jefferson died on July 4, 1826, the 50th anniversary of the signing of the Declaration of Independence.

FAST FACT

The Library of Congress, which now has more than 20 million books, was started with the purchase of Thomas Jefferson's personal library of 6,000 books.

Jefferson's Accomplishments

Pick out the one thing that Thomas Jefferson did not accomplish. Solution, see page 138.

1. **Wrote the Declaration of Independence**
2. **Organized the Lewis and Clark Expedition**
3. **Acquired the Louisiana Purchase**
4. **Invented the lightning rod**
5. **Founded the University of Virginia**

jellyfish

Marine animal with a pulsating jelly, bell-shaped body and trailing tentacles. It has no skeleton, no head, and no brain. The jellyfish is mostly water, with only about 1 percent living matter. The stings of some jellyfish can be deadly to humans.

JOAN OF ARC

At the age of 17, Joan of Arc (c. 1412 – 1431) heard "voices" that told her to save the kingdom of France from English domination. After several victories, she was captured, tried for heresy, and burned at the stake at the age of 19. Centuries later, she was made a saint by the Roman Catholic Church.

Jones, Casey

Casey Jones (1863 –1900) was a railroad engineer who drove the Cannon Ball Express from Memphis, Tennessee, to Canton, Mississippi. He became a folk hero when the Cannon Ball Express collided with a freight train on April 30, 1900. Rather than jump, Jones stayed in the cab and applied the brakes. He was killed, but his brave actions saved the passengers and crew.

Casey Jones

judo

A hand-to-hand sport that uses leverage, balance, and timing to turn an opponent's strength against him or her. It is a modified and less violent form of the Japanese martial art jujitsu. Participants wear colored belts that show their degree of mastery.

FAST FACT

"Judo" means "gentle way" in Japanese.

Don't Let This Throw You

The clues will help you figure out the answers. Then read the shaded letters in the answers to find the secret word. Solution, see page 138.

1. Original martial art   ☐ _ _ _ _ _ _
2. Contest referee   _ ☐ _ _ _ _
3. Type of sport   _ _ _ ☐ - _ - _ _ _ _
4. What each contest begins with   _ ☐ _

Secret word: _ _ _ _

juggler

An entertainer who keeps several objects in the air at the same time through expert throwing and catching. Ancient Egypt, Greece, and Rome had jugglers. Jugglers became popular features in fairs, circuses, and even the musical stage. Early movie comedian W. C. Fields began his career as a juggler and was a hit on Broadway.

Jupiter

Jupiter is larger than all the other planets in the solar system combined. It is the fourth-brightest object in the sky, after the sun, moon, and Venus. Jupiter has 16 moons. The largest moons, Callisto and Ganymede, are larger than the planet Mercury. Jupiter has the strongest magnetic field of all the planets, making it a giant magnet.

jump rope

Jump rope can be played alone or as a team game. As a team game, two people turn the rope in a circle while the others chant or count while taking turns jumping. Some of the chants are more than 200 years old, and have even been passed down from mother to daughter.

Prize-fighters and other athletes jump rope to develop their lungs and legs.

· ·

Looking Juggled

Which juggler is different from the others? Solution, see page 138.

Kalahari Desert

A 100,000-square-mile desert in southern Africa. It gets no more than 8 inches of rain a year. Daytime temperatures range between 95° to 113° Fahrenheit. They can drop to freezing between June and August. The desert is home to a great variety of animals, including the giraffe, hyena, and antelope. Diamonds were discovered in the Kalahari in 1971.

kangaroo

Kangaroos are marsupial mammals, animals that carry their young in pouches. The kangaroo's body is specially built for jumping, with large and strong hind legs and feet, and a large tail. It can leap along the ground at more than 30 miles an hour. A large kangaroo can travel up to 16 feet in a single leap.

When chased, a kangaroo will sometimes try to escape by jumping into a stream. But when cornered, the kangaroo will fight back. A large kangaroo balances on its tail and kicks with its back feet. One of the toes on each hind foot has a sharp claw. The kangaroo can rip a small animal to death with one stroke.

Khan, Genghis

Genghis Khan (1162–1227) was the Mongol conqueror who created one of the largest empires ever known. It included Iran, Afghanistan, and southern Russia, and stretched from China to Europe's Adriatic Sea.

Genghis Khan

Kidd, Captain William

William Kidd (c. 1645–1701) was commissioned by the
British governor of New York as a privateer, getting paid for
any French ships he seized. Off the East African coast,
Kidd turned to piracy. In 1701, he was hanged for piracy in
London. Some of his treasure was later dug up in
Gardiner's Island, near Long Island, New York.

Secret Pirate Bits

*The names of five famous pirates are hidden in the bits of
words below. Part of their first name is over part of their last
name. Who's the pirate in each bit of words? Solution, see
page 138.*

APT	EAN	OHN	RAN	NRY
IDD	AFI	KIN	RAK	RGA
1.	2.	3.	4.	5.

killer whale

A killer whale, or orca, is about 30 feet long. It is the largest member of the dolphin family. The killer whale is so named because it hunts fish, seabirds, sea turtles, and even whales two or three times its size. It is highly intelligent and uses many different sounds, including whistles and clicks, to communicate.

kite

A kite is a light frame covered with paper that soars in a steady breeze at the end of a line. It should not be flown on rainy days or near power lines. Kites were used in experiments by both Benjamin Franklin and Alexander Graham Bell, inventor of the telephone.

knight

At one time, a knight was a high military rank. The knight fought on horseback, using lance and sword, and wore heavy metal armor for protection. Today, knighthood is a special honor in Great Britain. It carries with it the title of "sir."

koala

The koala is a marsupial that lives in Australia. It feeds at night, mostly on the leaves of the

koala

eucalyptus tree. Like other marsupials, baby koalas live in their mother's pouch. Koalas get most of the water they need from eucalyptus leaves.

FAST FACT

Baby koalas are called joeys.

Knight Time

Each clue across is the name of something connected with a knight. When you write all the answers in the boxes, the name of something else connected with a knight will pop up in the shaded column going down. We've solved the first one to help you begin. Solution, see page 138.

ACROSS

1. Knight's shirt
2. Knight's transport
3. Knight's assistant
4. Knight's title
5. Knight's boss
6. Knight's weapon
7. Knight's protection
8. Knight of the Round Table
9. Knight's riding position
10. Knight's head gear

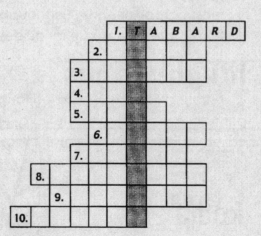

SHADED COLUMN

Knight's contest

Ladybug

A little beetle that feeds on insect pests. The ladybug is usually yellow or red in color with black spots. It is also called lady beetle or ladybird.

ladybug

lake

A large inland body of still water. It is larger than a pond. Some lakes, like Crater Lake in Oregon, were ancient volcanic craters that filled with water.

landslide

A rapid movement down a mountain slope of a mass of rock or earth. Earthquakes and volcanic eruptions sometimes cause landslides.

laughing gas

Nitrous oxide (N_2O) is called laughing gas. It is used in dentistry as a weak anesthetic to relieve pain. It was called laughing gas because it may bring on a fit of laughter when it is inhaled.

lava

Lava is red-hot liquid rock that erupts from a volcano or from a crack in the earth's surface. It can sometimes flow for a considerable distance. Its temperature is about 2,000° Fahrenheit.

lemur

A lemur is a monkey-like mammal with a sharp, pointed face, large eyes, very soft fur, and a long, furry tale. Lemurs live in trees on the island of Madagascar, off the east coast of Africa.

FAST FACT

> In 1844, Horace Wells became the first dentist to use nitrous oxide. He used it on himself before he had a tooth pulled.

Wet Puzzle

To solve the Wet Puzzle, fill in the answers to the clues, using one letter on each blank. Then transfer the letters to the boxes that have the same numbers. When all the boxes are filled in, you will find the answer to the Wet Puzzle. (Hint: Don't feel Superior. These are not small ponds.) Solution, see page 138.

A. _ _ _   Barrel
   8 3 1

B. _ _ _   Sticky black stuff
   5 7 2

C. _ _ _ _   Walrus kin
   10 9 4 6

1	2	3	4	5		6	7	8	9	10

lightning

Lightning is a flash of light in the sky. It is produced by a discharge of high-voltage electricity from a thundercloud. A flash can range from a few miles to about 100 miles long. Its temperature can reach 55,000° Fahrenheit.

Lincoln, Abraham

Abraham Lincoln (1809–1865) was the 16th president of the United States. While preserving the Union during the Civil War, he issued the Emancipation Proclamation, freeing all slaves in rebel states. He also signed the Homestead Act, which gave 160 acres to settlers who farmed the land for five years. Lincoln was assassinated five days after the end of the Civil War.

lizard

A lizard is a reptile, like snakes, alligators, and turtles. A lizard is a swift-moving hunter. It has sharp claws for catching its prey. Its long tail helps with balance. Chameleons, iguanas, monitors, and geckos are lizards. The largest living lizard is the 300-pound Komodo dragon. While most lizards are harmless, there are several poisonous lizards, including the Gila monster.

chameleon

llama

The llama is a long-eared mammal found in South America. It is distantly related to the camel. It has been used as a beast of burden in the Andes for 4,000 years. Because the blood of the llama has been adapted to the thin air of the mountains where it lives, it can work harder for longer periods.

 FAST FACT

> At six feet, four inches tall, Abraham Lincoln was the tallest president.

Lots of Lizards

Match each number to the letter in the code below to find the lizard names. Solution, see page 138.

A	B	C	D	E	F	G	H	I	J	K	L	M
1	2	3	4	5	6	7	8	9	10	11	12	13

N	O	P	Q	R	S	T	U	V	W	X	Y	Z
14	15	16	17	18	19	20	21	22	23	24	25	26

a) 7 5 3 11 15 _____

b) 13 15 14 9 20 15 18 _____

c) 9 7 21 1 14 1 _____

d) 3 8 1 13 5 12 5 15 14 _____

Manga

"Manga" is the term used to describe Japanese comic books and graphic novels. The characters drawn in the manga style usually have big, wide eyes. In Japan, everyone reads manga, including adults. Manga books for boys are called *shonen manga*. Manga books for girls are called *shojo manga*. Manga dates back to the 800s in Japan.

marsupial

Marsupials are a group of mammals that usually have a pouch on the abdomen of the female, which holds the young. Marsupials include the kangaroo, koala, wombat, and opossum. There are almost 300 species of marsupials. Most marsupials are found in Australia and New Zealand. One species, the Virginia opossum, lives in North America.

martial arts

Martial arts are systems of combat and self-defense that were developed in East Asia and are now widely practiced as sport. They include karate, aikido, tae kwan do, kendo, kung fu, jujitsu, and judo.

Mayflower

On September 21, 1620, the *Mayflower* carried the Pilgrims to America from Plymouth, England. It reached Provincetown, Massachusetts, on November 21, 500 miles north of the intended destination in Virginia. After the Pilgrims signed the Mayflower Compact, they sailed on to Plymouth, Massachusetts. The *Mayflower* was a ship with two decks. It weighed about 175 tons and was only 90 feet long. It held 102 people.

FAST FACT

Artist Tezuka Osamu is credited with revolutionizing the look of manga with such creations as Astro Boy, which went on to become a popular cartoon show.

Draw Your Own Manga Character

Draw your own version of a manga character to go along with this one.

meteorite

A piece of rock or metal from space that reaches the surface of the earth without being completely burned up. Meteorites are thought to be pieces of asteroids, small bodies that orbit the sun.

microscope

This instrument makes images of small objects appear larger by magnifying them. This means that things that are too small to be seen with the unaided eye can be easily viewed. Before the invention of the microscope, we knew little about tiny creatures such as bacteria.

microscope

Middle Ages

This was the period in Europe from the 5th to the 15th century. It was a very important time. At the beginning of the Middle Ages, the western half of the Roman Empire broke up into smaller, weaker kingdoms. By the end of the Middle Ages, many modern European countries were taking shape. It was also the beginning of institutions, such as universities, that are still with us today.

The Middle East holds nearly 70 percent of the world's oil reserves.

Middle East

The Middle East is the large region that includes the countries extending from Libya in North Africa to Afghanistan in Southwest Asia. The Middle East was the home of early civilization. It was also the birthplace of Judaism, Christianity, and Islam. It has been the home of many great empires.

Middle East Spell

There is one incorrectly spelled word in each group below. Can you find it? Solution, see page 139.

1.
a) Damascus
b) Tel Aviv
c) Bagdhad
d) Amman

2.
a) Oman
b) Lebenon
c) Iraq
d) Jordan

3.
a) Kerd
b) Sunni
c) Shia
d) Bedouin

4.
a) Caliph
b) Shiek
c) Sultan
d) Ayatollah

Milky Way

This is our home galaxy, holding the solar system. The Milky Way contains more than 100 billion stars. The Milky Way was named because at night it looks like a hazy, milk-like band of stars stretching across the sky.

Mongol Empire

The Mongol Empire united almost all of Asia in the 13th and 14th centuries. It was one of the largest empires in history. The Mongols were fierce warriors from what is today Inner Mongolia. Under Genghis Khan and later rulers, their empire stretched from what is now China and Korea in the east to Eastern Europe and the shores of the Mediterranean Sea in the west.

MONGOOSE

Playful and agile, the ferret-like mongoose is famous for attacking large and poisonous snakes. The mongoose is not immune to snake venom, but its thick coat helps protects it against a snake's fangs.

mongoose

The word "galaxy" itself comes from the Greek word for "milk."

monkey

One of about 160 species of primates that have grasping hands, forward-facing eyes, and highly developed brains. Most monkeys also have tails. They are very good climbers, and most spend much of their lives in trees.

Montezuma

Montezuma (1466–1520) was the last Aztec emperor of Mexico. He believed the Spaniards to be white gods, refused to fight them, and was taken hostage. The Aztecs rebelled, and Montezuma was killed while trying to negotiate with the Spaniards.

Monkey Business

Can you identify these "monkey" words from the clues?
Solution, see page 139.

1. **This six-letter word starts with M and ends with Y, and it means "to fool around or to tamper with."** _____

2. **This three-letter word starts with A and ends with E, and it means "to imitate or copy."** _____

3. **This seven-letter word starts with G and ends with A, and it means "a thug."** _____

moon

The only natural satellite of Earth, the moon has no atmosphere or water. It is held in place by Earth's gravity. Every 28 days or so, the moon passes through a series of phases by waxing (growing) to a new moon, through the first quarter, to full moon, then waning (shrinking) to the last quarter and new moon again. This gives us our month.

mountain

A mountain is a landmass that rises very steeply above its surroundings. Most mountains are part of a chain, group, or range. Important mountain systems include the Rockies (North America), the Andes (South America), Himalayas (Asia), and the Alps (Europe).

Mount Everest

Mount Everest is the highest point on Earth. It is 29,028 feet high, on the border between Nepal and Tibet in the Himalayas. Tibetans call Mount Everest *Chomolungma*, or "Goddess Mother of the World." Many unsuccessful attempts were made to climb to the top of Mount Everest. On May 29, 1953, Sir Edmund Hillary of New Zealand and his Nepalese Sherpa guide, Tenzing Norgay, became the first people to reach the top of Mount Everest.

Mount Rushmore

Mount Rushmore is a granite cliff that has carved into it the faces of four American presidents: George Washington, Thomas Jefferson, Theodore Roosevelt, and

Abraham Lincoln. Mount Rushmore is located in the Black Hills of South Dakota. Mount Rushmore was designed by Gutzon Borglum. Work on the supersize sculpture began in 1927, and was not completed until more than 14 years later. Borglum died before it was complete.

FAST FACT

> The head of George Washington on Mount Rushmore is as big tall as a five-story building, or about 60 feet high.

Add a President to Mount Rushmore

Draw in the president you think should be added to Mount Rushmore.

$\mathcal{N}$apoléon

Napoléon Bonaparte (1769–1821) was emperor of France and for a brief time ruled most of Europe. He introduced educational and legal reforms to France, many of which are still in place, and invaded Russia. After being defeated at Waterloo, he was exiled to St. Helena, a small island 1,200 miles west of Africa.

NASCAR

NASCAR is the organization that governs stock car racing in the United States. NASCAR stands for the National Association for Stock Car Racing. NASCAR was founded in 1947, and the first real NASCAR race was held in Charlotte, North Carolina, in 1949.

Neptune

The eighth planet from the sun, Neptune is named for the Roman god of water. In fact, most of the planet is supposed to be a deep ocean. Neptune is 2.8 billion miles from the sun. It takes Neptune 165 Earth years to orbit the sun.

FAST FACT

Neptune has eight moons.

Nero

Nero (37–68 AD) was a cruel and unstable emperor of Rome. When his reign became increasingly violent and insane, he was declared a public enemy of the

Senate. Deserted by his bodyguard, he committed suicide on June 9, 68 AD.

Nile

The Nile River is the longest river in the world. It is 4,160 miles long. It flows north, from central Africa to the Mediterranean. Fertile silt deposited by the Nile's annual overflow made ancient Egypt a prosperous land.

....

Start Your Engines!

Help this race car driver reach the finish line first. Solution, see page 139.

nitroglycerin

This colorless, oily liquid is a very powerful high explosive. When detonated, it produces about 10,000 times its own volume of gas. It is 13 times as powerful as gunpowder. Because it is very sensitive to shock, it is unsafe to use in its normal state. Even moving it can set it off. The Swedish inventor Alfred Nobel used it to make dynamite, a less sensitive and safer explosive. When used today, nitroglycerin is usually mixed with sawdust or other absorbents.

nomad

A person with no fixed residence who moves from place to place. Nomads move according to the seasons within a well-defined territory, in search of food, water, and grazing land. They include herdsmen such as the Bedouins of North Africa, and the Sami of Scandinavia. In ancient times, semi-nomadic peoples such as Goths, Huns, and Vandals would move through Europe, sometimes settling down, other times moving on.

Bedouins

Nitroglycerin is also used to treat certain heart conditions.

Norman Conquest

In 1066, the Normans invaded and conquered England. The Normans were the descendants of Vikings who had previously conquered Normandy, a part of present-day France. The land of England was redistributed among the conquerors, and Norman feudalism became the basis of law. England got new French-speaking rulers and a new social and political structure.

....

On the Move

The names of various peoples have gotten mixed up. Rearrange the letters and write their correct names in the blanks. We've put all the Ds and Gs in their names in their proper places to start you off. The circled letters will spell out an activity common to all these peoples. Put those letters in the blanks for the Mystery Word. Solution, see page 139.

1. **Thogs**   G _ ◯ _ _

2. **Mornans**   _ _ ◯ _ _ _

3. **Smadon**   _ _ _ ◯ D _

4. **Skiving**   ◯ _ _ _ _ G _

5. **Soudebin**   _ ◯ D _ _ _ _

6. **Splap**   ◯ _ _ _ _

Mystery Word   _ _ _ _ _ _

79

North Pole

The most northern point on Earth is called the North Pole. There are really two North Poles: the geographic and the magnetic North Poles. The geographic North Pole lies roughly at the center of the Arctic Ocean and is the north-ernmost point of our planet. From the North Pole, all directions on Earth's surface are south.

The magnetic North Pole is located in northern Canada, more than 1,000 miles from the geographic North Pole. The magnetic North Pole is pointed to by compasses. Because of the difference in distances between the two North Poles, compass readings always need to be corrected.

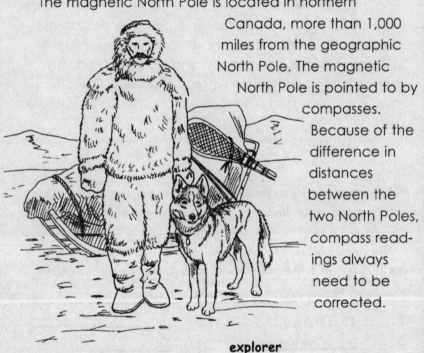

explorer

North Star

The North Star is also called the Polestar. This star, in the constellation Ursa Minor, appears to remain directly above Earth's North Pole. It never sets. You can see this same star from any place in the Northern Hemisphere. When you point to the North Star, you are pointing north. It is always in the same place in the sky. That's why sailors have always used the North Star to chart their voyages.

FAST FACT

Another name for the North Star is Polaris.

....

polar Words

Can you make 12 words using the letters in the words ARCTIC OCEAN? Solution, see page 140.

1. _____   7. _____

2. _____   8. _____

3. _____   9. _____

4. _____   10. _____

5. _____   11. _____

6. _____   12. _____

O ak

Oaks are among the most beautiful of trees. They grow slowly, but can grow to be 150 feet tall and live for 1,000 years. Their wood is strong, straight-grained, and very long-lasting. Cork is the thick outer bark of the cork oak, which grows in southern Europe and North Africa. The fruit of the oak is the acorn.

ocean

The world ocean—all the oceans together—covers 71 percent of Earth's surface. Its parts include the Pacific, the Atlantic, the Indian, and the Arctic Oceans, which cover almost 130 million square miles. Its average depth is 16,000 feet. The deepest part of the ocean is the Mariana Trench in the Pacific Ocean, which is almost 36,000 feet deep. The world ocean also includes the seas and gulfs around the borders of the oceans. These bodies of water are partially enclosed by land. They include the Mediterranean, Baltic, Caribbean, Black, Red, and North Seas, the Gulf of Mexico, and the Persian Gulf.

octopus

The octopus is found worldwide in tropical and warm, temperate waters. It lives on other sea animals such as moray eels, scallops, and small crabs. It is a smart and active hunter. The octopus has a soft, bag-shaped body. Its eyes are large and unblinking. It also has a well-

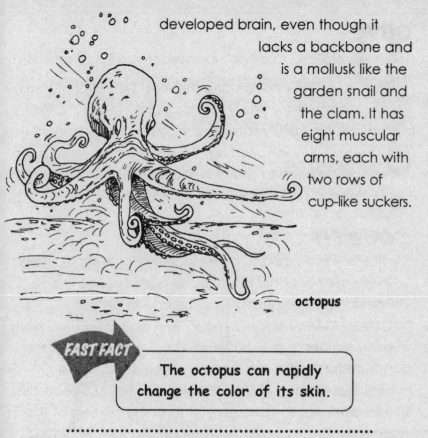

developed brain, even though it lacks a backbone and is a mollusk like the garden snail and the clam. It has eight muscular arms, each with two rows of cup-like suckers.

octopus

FAST FACT

The octopus can rapidly change the color of its skin.

Shade Tree

Z T Z A Z L Z
L Z O X A X K
X S X F X R Z
O Z M Z L Z I
Z T X T X L X
E X A X C X Z
O Z R Z N Z S
X G X R X O X
X Z X Z W Z X

Shade in all the letters that aren't Z or X, then read a proverb about growing up. Solution, see page 140.

olive

This evergreen tree from the Mediterranean is one of the world's oldest cultivated crops. Its fruits are eaten whole and are also pressed to make olive oil. An olive branch is an ancient symbol of peace.

OLYMPICS

The Olympic Games are held every four years in different cities around the world. They are a modern re-creation of the ancient Greek sporting contests, which had been banned in ad 394. The modern games were started in 1896, by a French scholar who was inspired by the ancient Greek games.

Olympic athlete

orchestra

An orchestra is organized into four basic groups: strings, woodwinds, brass, and percussion. In addition to these four groups, orchestras usually have a harp and a piano. An orchestra is directed by a conductor. A symphony orchestra performs symphonies and other concert music and is usually placed on a stage.

ostrich

At almost 9 feet high and weighing 325 pounds, the ostrich is the largest living bird. The ostrich cannot fly, but can run 40 miles per hour. Ostriches live in groups in East Africa.

FAST FACT

Three-pound ostrich eggs are the largest living, single-celled organisms in the world.

The Words of Music

Rearrange these musical words or phrases to make new words or phrases. For instance, rearrange a musical threesome to make a mob scene. Answer: Trio > Riot. Solution, see page 140.

1. Rearrange "supersonic" to make a part of an orchestra.

----

2. Rearrange "silent" to make what an audience should do.

----

3. Rearrange "deer" to make an oboe.

----

4. Rearrange "groan" to make a church instrument.

----

otter

The otter is a member of the weasel family that lives in dens along the water. It is social, playful, agile, and intelligent. Otters can spend hours just sliding down the side of a mud bank, like kids on a playground slide. The sea otter floats on its back, breaking open the shellfish it eats on a stone that it balances on its chest.

owl

A bird of prey whose eyesight is 100 times sharper than ours. The flight of the owl is completely silent because of its soft feathers. The owl's flexible neck allows its head to turn 270 degrees—almost a complete circle! Owls hunt by night.

owl

oxygen

A gaseous element that has no color, odor, or taste. It is the most abundant element found on Earth. As a gas it makes up 20 percent of the world's atmosphere. In combination with hydrogen it makes up 90 percent of all water. Oxygen is necessary for life and is found in all living matter.

oyster

Oysters are shellfish living in shallow coastal waters. Some oysters produce valuable pearls, while other oysters are valued as a food delicacy. The oyster lives its life cemented to a hard rock, feeding on food flowing its way through currents.

 FAST FACT

The giant otter of South American can reach five feet in length.

Common Cause

What do they have in common? Every item in a group shares something with the other items in the group. Can you identify what it may be? Solution, see page 140.

1. Otter
   Polecat
   Badger
   Wolverine
   Mink
   Ferret

2. Oxygen
   Nitrogen
   Argon
   Carbon dioxide
   Neon
   Helium
   Methane
   Water vapor

3. Owl
   Leopard
   Moray eel
   Bat
   Opossum
   Hippopotamus

Pacific Ocean

The Pacific Ocean is the largest ocean. It extends from the Arctic Circle to Antarctica, and from western North and South America to East Asia and Australia. It is almost 70 million square miles in size.

palm tree

A valuable tree found in the tropics and subtropics. Different varieties provide coconuts, dates, edible oils, and waxes. The palm leaf is traditionally a symbol of victory or rejoicing.

Panama Canal

The waterway across the Isthmus of Panama connecting the Atlantic and Pacific oceans. The United States built it, from 1904 to 1914, at a cost of $380 million. Before the building of the Panama Canal, a voyage between New York City and San Francisco took 7,900 miles longer, because the ship had to sail around the tip of South America.

PANDA

There are two kinds of panda. The 250-pound giant panda is a member of the bear family. The lesser panda, which is about the size of a large cat, is thought to be related to the raccoon. Pandas are found in bamboo forests in the Himalayas and central and western China. Giant pandas spend up to 14 hours a day eating bamboo, about 40 pounds a day.

parachute

The parachute was invented in the late 18th century. Shaped like an umbrella, it slows a person down while he or she falls through the air.

Once the parachute opens, the jumper descends at a rate of about 17 feet per second. A parachutist will hit the ground with about the same

parachutist

force as if he or she had jumped from a 10-foot wall.

Endangered Species Search

Unscramble the letters to find the endangered species.
Solution, see page 140.

thacehe _____

riglalo _____

tinag danap _____

grunatona _____

grite _____

Only about 1,000 giant pandas
remain in the world.

parrot

More than 340 species of brightly colored birds make up the parrot family. Parrots have curved, hooked bills, and short legs. Their first and fourth toes are turned backward. They walk awkwardly but are excellent climbers, using their bills to pull themselves up to higher branches. Many parrots can imitate the human voice.

parrot

Pasteur, Louis

Louis Pasteur (1822–1895) was a French chemist and one of the founders of the science of microbiology (the study of microorganisms and their effects). He developed a vaccine for rabies. He also invented the process of pasteurization, a heating process that kills harmful bacteria in milk.

peanut

Peanuts originated in South America. The peanut is an unusual plant because its fruit or pod develops in the ground. About half the peanuts grown in the United States are made into peanut butter, and one-fourth are sold as roasted peanuts. George Washington Carver, the noted agricultural scientist, developed hundreds of uses for peanuts.

Who Am I?

Can you guess the invention and idea and who was responsible for it? Match the invention and the inventor from the lists below and write them in the spaces given. Solution, see page 140.

Solution, see page 140.

	What was it?	Who did it?
1. My invention pulls sparks out of the sky and makes buildings safe.	_____	_____
2. My invention goes to the highest places.	_____	_____
3. My invention makes milk safe to drink.	_____	_____
4. My ideas turned a plant into a gold mine.	_____	_____

Invention	Inventor
Uses for the peanut	Benjamin Franklin
Pasteurization	Elisha Otis
Elevator	Louis Pasteur
Lightning Rod	George Washington Carver

PELICAN

These large birds have a long, large, flattened bill with an expandable pouch attached to the lower jaw. The pouch is used to catch fish, not store them for later eating. The brown pelican is the state bird of Louisiana.

Phoenicians

Phoenicians gave civilization the alphabet and glassmaking. Phoenicia was a 200-mile-long strip of semi-independent city-states on the eastern coast of the Mediterranean Sea, in a region now in modern Lebanon and Syria. The most important of these city-states were Tyre and Sidon. Phoenicians were great sailors and traders. They founded many colonies, including Utica and Carthage in North Africa, and the islands of Rhodes and Cyprus in the Mediterranean.

Phoenician sailing ship

pigeon

The wild ancestor of the pigeon is the rock dove. There are more than 200 domestic breeds of common pigeon. One of them is the street or feral pigeon, found in cities all over the world. Other breeds include the homing pigeon and the carrier pigeon. Some pigeons are called doves. The most common North American dove is the mourning dove, named for its sad call.

FAST FACT The passenger pigeon has been extinct since 1914. Before then, millions of passenger pigeons would migrate north in the spring in flocks large enough to darken the sky.

Pigeon Coop

In each sentence below, the word "pigeon" has been substituted for a common word. "Pigeon" stands for the same word in each statement. Try to discover what "pigeon" is before you get to number 5. Solution, see page 140.

1. When it's cold, some "pigeons" may need protection. In Alaska, it's important to have a "pigeon" warmer.

2. Try to keep your "pigeon," even though others may be losing theirs.

3. Take care not to fall "pigeon" over heels, because you may be almost helpless.

4. When you've arrived at the correct solution, you've hit the nail on the "pigeon," so go to the "pigeon" of the class.

5. Two "pigeons" are better than one.

planet

A planet is a large body in space that orbits a star and shines by reflected light. In our solar system, there are nine planets that orbit the sun: Mercury, Venus, Earth, Mars, Jupiter, Saturn, Uranus, Neptune, and Pluto. Planets that orbit stars other than the sun are called extra-solar planets. Smaller bodies that also orbit a star and are not satellites of a planet are called asteroids.

FAST FACT

The call of the foot-long platypus is a low growl.

platypus

One of the oddest creatures on the planet is the duck-billed platypus of eastern Australia and Tasmania. It is a mammal, yet it lays eggs like a bird or reptile. It has a sensitive duck bill that it uses to sniff out the worms and other small animals that it eats. Its feet are webbed, and there are poisonous spurs on the ankles of its hind feet. The platypus has keen senses of sight and hearing.

polar bear

Feeding mainly on seals, the 1,800-pound polar bear inhabits the frozen north. Female polar bears give birth while in hibernation. While hunting on ice, white polar bears will hide their black noses with their paws as a form of camouflage. Polar bears swim with their heads and shoulders above water.

Pony Express

The Pony Express was a mail service operating 2,000 miles across the West from 1860 to 1861. It used relays of horses and riders to deliver the mail in 10 days between Saint Joseph, Missouri, and Sacramento, California. Only one mail delivery was ever lost.

quicksand

Heavy objects easily sink in quicksand, which is a deep mass of loose sand saturated with water. Quicksand is dangerous because it resembles regular sand.

The Pony Express Rides Again!

Help this Pony Express rider deliver the mail. He needs to find his way from Saint Joseph, Missouri, to Sacramento, California. Solution, see page 141.

Raccoon

Raccoons will eat anything from fish and frogs to seeds and nuts. A raccoon's front paws and nose are very sensitive. While a raccoon may weigh as much as 45 pounds, in the winter months, it may lose as much as 50 percent of its body weight.

raccoon

radium

The husband-and-wife scientist team of Pierre and Marie Curie discovered the radioactive element radium in 1898. Radium is used to treat certain cancers.

Rain

We get rain when water vapor in the atmosphere condenses and forms clouds. The water droplets grow in size and finally fall. The heaviest annual rainfall in the United States is in the Southeast, where the average may be up to 70 inches a year. More than 450 inches a year falls at Cherrapunji in northeastern India. This is the world's heaviest average rainfall. The town has received more than 785 inches of rain in one year.

rainbow

When sunlight passes through raindrops, spray, mist, or even a waterfall, a colored arc, or rainbow, is formed, which shows all the colors of the spectrum. The colors in a rainbow are violet, blue, green, yellow, orange, and red.

FAST FACT

Small, falling raindrops are called drizzle.

Rainy Expressions

Complete the expression by matching the right phrase.
Solution, see page 141.

1. Raining   A. April

2. Take a rain   B. pours

3. Come rain or   C. cats and dogs

4. When it rains, it   D. shine

5. showers   E. check

rap music

Rap music is a type of music that is usually spoken at a fast pace. Rap is performed along to music that stresses rhythm over melody. Rap songs also sometimes use bits of other prerecorded songs to make new songs. This is called sampling. Rap music became popular in New York City, in the mid-1970s, and soon caught on across the country.

rattlesnake

A widespread, highly poisonous pit viper. It has a tail rattle that is shaken as a threat or warning. The rattlesnake's rattle can be heard up to 30 miles away.

Rattlesnakes can grow to 8 feet long. Rattlesnakes can strike from any position, even while slithering forward on the ground. Bites to humans are not uncommon; however, deaths are rare in the United States because toxin-fighting antivenims are easily obtainable.

rattlesnake

The most dangerous rattlesnake is the Cascavael of South America—75 percent of its human victims die of asphyxiation.

reptile

Air-breathing vertebrates with tough, dry skin covered with horny scales. Reptiles include alligators and crocodiles, lizards, snakes, turtles, and thousands of extinct species. Modern reptiles range in size from species of tiny snakes and lizards with lengths of less than two inches to crocodiles, pythons, and anacondas that grow to more than 30 feet long.

In contrast to birds and mammals, reptiles are cold-blooded. They warm or cool themselves by moving to warmer or cooler locations. Most become dormant under cold conditions.

FAST FACT

One of the first rap groups was the Sugar Hill Gang. They had a hit in 1979 with "Rapper's Delight."

Reptile House

In the group below, complete each word to form the names of six reptiles. Next, take each numbered letter and place it on the same numbered blanks of the Mystery Word. When you are done, you should have an eight-letter name of a very large reptile. Solution, see page 141.

1. _ L L I _ A T O _
   1   3

2. C R O C _ D I L E
        4

3. L I _ _ R _
        7

4. S N _ K _
   2 8

5. T _ R _ L E

6. P _ _ _ O N
       5 6

Mystery Word _ _ _ _ _ _ _ _
          1 2 3 4 5 6 7 8

river

A natural inland stream of water flowing downhill along a channel. It begins at an upland source and empties into a lake or sea at its mouth. Smaller rivers called tributaries may join it along the way. Rivers shape the land, wearing down the rock in some places and redepositing it in others.

robot

Robots are computer-controlled machines that can often perform repetitive tasks faster and more accurately than humans.

The word "robot" comes from the Czech word for "work." It was first used by the playwright Karel Capek in his 1921 science-fiction play *R.U.R.* Science-fiction writers have also invented imaginary creations called androids, which are robots that look human, and cyborgs, which are bionic humans, such as those in *Robocop* and the *Terminator* movies.

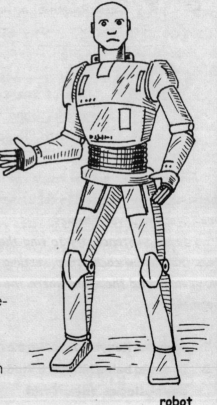

robot

rock music

Rock music, often called rock 'n' roll, is a popular form of music that dates back to the mid-1950s. Rock music developed mainly from two other forms of American music, country and Western, and blues.

> **FAST FACT**
>
> Many rock historians consider "Rocket 88," by Jackie Brenston, to be the first rock 'n' roll song. The song was about a type of car called an Oldsmobile.

· ·

Hidden Rivers

Find the river hidden inside the sentence, "Clean up, Martha—messiness is not wanted." Look closely at "Martha—messiness," and you'll find the river Thames.

In each sentence, try to find the American river hidden in letters that follow each other, reading left to right. To help you, we've indicated the state where the river is found. Solution, see page 141.

1. **Does the Kenya zoo feature a rhino? (Mississippi)**
2. **To avoid being hit with a thud, sonar will warn the ship of any obstacles. (New York)**
3. **Use the mop to swab ashes and other dirt off the deck. (Indiana)**
4. **Some people eat swan, eels, and octopus. (Georgia)**

Sacagawea

Sacagawea (c. 1787–1812) was a Shoshone Native American. She was of great assistance to the Lewis and Clark Expedition from 1805 to 1806. Her presence proved to other Native

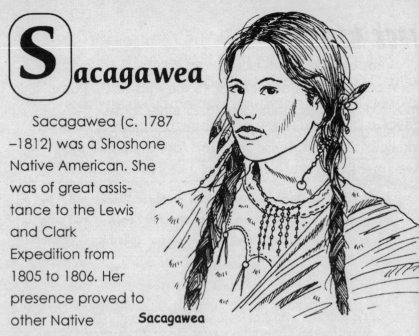

Sacagawea

Americans that the expedition had peaceful intentions. She was an interpreter and guide. She also saved navigational instruments, trade goods, and valuable journals when one of the expedition's boats nearly capsized.

salt

Salt gave us our word "salary." Originally, this word meant "salt money." It was the allowance of salt paid to Roman soldiers. Salt was precious to ancient people. Salt cakes were used as currency in Ethiopia and Tibet. "To eat salt" was to agree to a covenant or bond. Salt is still a valuable commodity today. We use it to preserve and flavor food, but it is necessary for health as well. When we use the word "salt," we usually mean table salt (sodium chloride), but it can also refer to other compounds as well.

satellites

Natural satellites are small bodies that revolve around a larger astronomical object, like the moons circling the planets of the solar system. Man-made objects that revolve around a larger astronomical object are called artificial satellites. These are used for communication, weather study, navigation, and military surveillance.

FAST FACT

In 2000, the U.S. Mint honored Sacagawea's memory by issuing a dollar coin with her likeness.

Salty Words

Can you figure out these words that all begin with SAL? Solution, see page 141.

1. **Wages**   S A L _ _ _
2. **Salty**   S A L _ _ _
3. **Type of sausage**   S A L _ _ _
4. **Spicy condiment**   S A L _ _
5. **Greens**   S A L _ _

Saturn

The planet Saturn is a gas giant composed mostly of hydrogen and helium. It is covered with cloud bands. Because it takes nearly 30 years to revolve around the sun, the ancients named it

Saturn

Saturn, after the elderly, slow-moving father of the gods in mythology. Saturn is surrounded by a beautiful ring system that can be easily seen with any small telescope.

sea horse

This fish looks like the chess piece called a knight. Its head and neck are shaped like a horse's and it swims upright, very slowly and not very gracefully. Its long tail can grasp objects such as seaweed.

Secret Service

The Secret Service is the oldest general law enforcement agency of the federal government. It was created in 1865 as a branch of the Department of the Treasury to fight counterfeiting and smuggling. In 2002, it was made part of the Department of Homeland Security.

While the Secret Service investigates cases of counterfeiting and forgery, it also provides personal protection to high government officials, including the president, the vice-president, and their families, as well as certain other people.

FAST FACT

There is a Secret Service Uniformed Division that guards the White House and other key residences.

The Puzzle of the Secret Service

To solve the Secret Service puzzle, fill in the answers to the clues, one letter on each blank. Then transfer the letters to the boxes above that have the same numbers. When all the boxes are filled in, you will find the answer to the Secret Service Puzzle. (Hint: The address is 1600 Pennsylvania Avenue.) Solution, see page 141.

1	2	3	4	5		6	7	8	9	10

A. _ _ _   **Smack**
   6 3 4

B. _ _ _   **Take to court**
   9 8 10

C. _ _ _ _   **Julia Ward _____, Battle Hymn**
   2 7 1 5   **of the Republic**

skeleton

The bones of the body form a framework called the skeleton. This framework supports and protects the soft tissues and organs of the body. All the higher animals have an internal skeleton with a central spine, or backbone. There are between 200 and 212 bones in the human skeleton, to which more than 500 muscles are attached.

Statue of Liberty

The Statue of Liberty is a giant copper sculpture that stands above Liberty Island at the entrance to New York Harbor near the island of Manhattan. The statue is 151 feet and 1 inch tall and weighs about 225 tons.

Statue of Liberty

The statue was a gift to the United States from France as a symbol of friendship and to celebrate liberty, a concept that was and is important to both countries. The statue was officially presented to the United States in 1884.

sunspots

These are large, dark spots on the surface of the sun caused by changes in the sun's magnetic field. Sunspots are more than 500 million square miles in size. They are easily visible with a telescope. Sunspots appear dark, because they are much cooler than their bright surroundings.

FAST FACT

The Statue of Liberty's complete name is Liberty Enlightening the World.

Find the Bones

Someone mislaid the bones from the anatomy class's skeleton. Shade in all the Qs, Ws, and Xs. Read the remaining letters from left to right, right to left, up and down, and down and up to find the bones. Solution, see page 142.

```
P W E L W V I W S X
A Q W W W W Q X X X
T I B I W A W Q W X
E X I W X W Q W Q X
L X R Q W Q W Q W X
L W L W U W K S X Q
A X F X E W M Q U R
```

Taj Mahal

In the city of Agra in northern India sits the Taj Mahal, one of the most beautiful buildings in the world. It is a mausoleum, or tomb, built by an emperor for his empress. Twenty

Taj Mahal

thousand workmen labored more than 20 years, from about 1632 to about 1653, to build this magnificent structure. The Taj Mahal is covered in pure white marble.

tank

Armored combat vehicle that runs on caterpillar tracks. The word "tank" was a code term for the first such machine, which was launched by the British in 1916, during the first World War.

TARANTULA

Giant hairy spider with enormous fangs that eats large insects and small vertebrates. The goliath tarantula of South America has a body length of 4 inches and a leg span of up to 10 inches. Some tarantulas produce a hissing sound. The tarantula's bite, while painful, is usually not deadly.

tea

Tea is brewed from the cured and dried young leaves and leaf buds of the tea plant, produced by 30 countries, including China, India, Indonesia, Sri Lanka, and Japan. Tea has been drunk in China for many centuries, perhaps as far back as 2700 BC. The Dutch brought tea to Europe in the early 1600s. England soon became a country of tea drinkers. Early European settlers introduced tea into North America.

FAST FACT

> The center dome of the Taj Mahal is
> more than 240 feet tall.

Tanks A Lot

Unscramble all the words below to learn the name of the famous British statesman who, in 1916, first recommended the use of the tank in warfare. Solution, see page 142.

inswton hillchurc

_____

teeth

Teeth are made mainly of dentine, covered with enamel. Enamel is the hardest substance in the body. Well-preserved teeth have been found from humans and other animals that lived thousands of years ago.

Adult humans have 32 teeth—16 in the upper jaw and 16 in the lower jaw—that work together to chew food. These include 8 incisors in the front of the mouth that cut food; 4 canines that tear food; 8 bicuspids or premolars; and 12 molars that grind and mash food.

telescope

This optical device magnifies images of faint and distant objects. It is used in astronomy as well as on land and sea. There are two types of telescope: the refracting and the reflecting. The refracting type is a tube with lenses on either end. The reflecting type has a mirror that collects and focuses incoming light. Large astronomical telescopes are the reflecting type.

telescope

Humans have two sets of teeth during their lives. The first set is baby teeth. These teeth are gradually replaced by the permanent teeth.

"Ain't It the Tooth?"

Use a simple reversed alphabet code (A = Z, B = Y, C =X) to decode this thought about teeth, written by the author of Don Quixote. To ease the pain of extracting the letters, we've pulled out all 26 letters and put them side-by-side with their opposite number. Each word is separated by a /. Now all you have to do is fill in the right letters. Solution, see page 142.

Z = A	M = N
Y = B	L = O
X = C	K = P
W = D	J = Q
V = E	I = R
U = F	H = S
T = G	G = T
S = H	F = U
R = I	E = V
Q = J	D = W
P = K	C = X
O = L	B = Y
N = M	A = Z

VEVIB/GLLGS/RM/Z/NZM'H/SVZW/RH/DLIGS/NLIV/

_ _ _ _ _ / _ _ _ _ _ / _ _ / _ / _ _ _ ' _ / _ _ _ _ / _ _ / _ _ _ _ _ / _ _ _ _ /

GSZM/Z/WRZNLMW

_ _ _ _ / _ / _ _ _ _ _ _ _ .

termites

Even though termites are related to cockroaches, they are often called "white ants," because they resemble ants. Just like ants, they live in large colonies with an elaborate social system. Different members of the group are assigned to different jobs as royalty, nobility, soldiers, and workers. Termites eat wood fiber or cellulose. While most animals can't digest cellulose, termites have a symbiotic relationship or partnership with microorganisms called protozoa which live in the gut of the termites. The protozoa transform cellulose so that termites can digest it.

FAST FACT

A termite colony may number more than one million termites.

Thanksgiving Day

This annual federal holiday is celebrated on the fourth Thursday in November. It commemorates a three-day harvest celebration held by the Pilgrims of Plymouth colony along with their Native American neighbors in 1621.

thermometer

An instrument for determining the temperature. It was first devised by Galileo around 1600. One type consists of a glass bulb containing a small reservoir of liquid, such as mercury or colored alcohol, which rises and falls with changes of temperature, measured with a numbered scale. Other types measure different temperature degrees on the Celsius and Fahrenheit scales, and in Kelvins.

thunder

An explosive sound wave produced when air suddenly expands upon being heated by a lightning discharge. It may be a sudden clap or a rumble for several seconds that changes in pitch and loudness. Echoes from hills can contribute to the rumbling sound. Light travels more quickly than sound, so lightning is first seen and then the thunder is heard, the sound traveling at about one mile every five seconds. That is why you can estimate, the distance, in miles, to be one-fifth the time in seconds between the lightning and thunder.

On the Way to the First Thanksgiving

Help these Wampanoag Native Americans make their way to the first Thanksgiving feast.

Solution, see page 142.

tides

Twice a day, the level of the sea changes. These changes are called high tide and low tide. Twice a month, tides (spring tides) are highest, when the moon is new or full; or lowest (neap tides), when the moon is in its first or third quarter. Tides are caused by the gravitational attraction of the moon and, to a lesser extent, of the sun.

tiger

The tiger is the largest of the big cats, with a 10-foot-long Bengal tiger weighing up to 550 pounds. Tigers are native to Asia. Tigers can jump up to 35 feet in one leap. A tiger's roar can be heard for a mile and a half away. Tigers hunt alone, mostly at night, traveling 5 to 15 miles in a night in search of prey. A tiger catches prey only once in 10 to 20 hunts. Tigers may become man-eaters when they lose the ability to kill their swifter natural prey.

tiger

trees

A plant is called a tree if it has a woody stem eight feet or more in height. The stem may not have branches for several feet above the ground. It is crowned at the top by branches and leaves. A tree's height and single main stem make it different from a shrub, which is shorter, and has many stems. There are two main groups of trees, coniferous and broad-leaved. Conifers bear cones. Their leaves are usually needle-shaped. They include pines, redwoods, and cypresses. Most conifers are evergreen. Their leaves last three or four years.

Trees of the second group have broad, flat leaves, like oaks and beeches. Most of them shed their leaves in winter to save water and are called deciduous.

FAST FACT

Trees are not found in deserts, on high mountaintops, or near the poles.

....

Branch Ranch and Other Po-e-TREE

If a place where you round up twigs is a branch ranch, what are the following? Just add the missing word to get a rhyme. Solution, see page 143.

1. An even-tempered tropical tree   _ _ _ _ palm
2. A hard-to-find fruit tree   _ _ _ _ pear
3. Asthmatic poplar   _ _ _ _ _ _ aspen
4. Looking for the best canoe bark   birch _ _ _ _ _ _

*U*ncle Sam

This nickname and cartoon symbolizes the U.S. government. The cartoon shows a thin, white-haired, bearded gentleman dressed in a high hat and old-fashioned tailed coat bearing the Stars and Stripes. It first appeared in the *New York Lantern*, a comic weekly, on March 13, 1852. In 1961, it was officially adopted as a national symbol.

Uncle Sam

Underground Railroad

For more than 40 years before the Civil War, this secret network through 14 states helped slaves escape from the South to the North and Canada. It was neither underground nor a railroad. It was named for its secrecy and for the railroading terms used to disguise the nature of its operation. For instance, "conductors" were the men and women, sometimes themselves former slaves, who led the slaves to safety. The freed slaves were called "freight," routes were called "lines," and isolated farms were "stations." The number of slaves, "freemen," who reached freedom through the

Underground Railroad may have been as high as 50,000. When the Civil War began in 1861, the "railroad" (which was also called the Liberty Line) closed down.

URANUS

The third-largest planet in our solar system, Uranus is the seventh from the sun, 1.9 billion miles away. Uranus was discovered in 1781 by the English brother and sister astronomers, William and Caroline Herschel. Because of its frozen methane atmosphere, it has a soft blue-green color. Uranus has 15 known moons. Uranus and its moons orbit around the sun tilted to one side. In 1977, Uranus was found to have rings like Saturn, only narrower and thinner.

FAST FACT

Uranus was the first planet to be discovered in modern times.

....

planetary Puzzle

Unscramble these words that have to do with the planet Uranus. Solution, see page 143.

1. omeranstro _ _ _ _ _ _ _ _ _ _
2. zenfro _ _ _ _ _ _
3. smono _ _ _ _ _
4. itobr _ _ _ _ _

VALLEY FORGE

This was the winter quarters of General George Washington and the encampment of the 11,000-man Continental Army on the Schulykill River, 22 miles northwest of Philadelphia, in the bleak winter of 1777 to 1778, during the Revolutionary War. A harsh winter and lack of adequate shelter, food, and supplies nearly destroyed the army. Soldiers were barefoot and without warm clothing in the bitter cold. More than 2,000 men died. During these darkest of hours, Baron Frederick William von Steuben trained, disciplined, drilled, and reorganized the army. In the spring, the Continental army emerged, well-disciplined, and battle-ready.

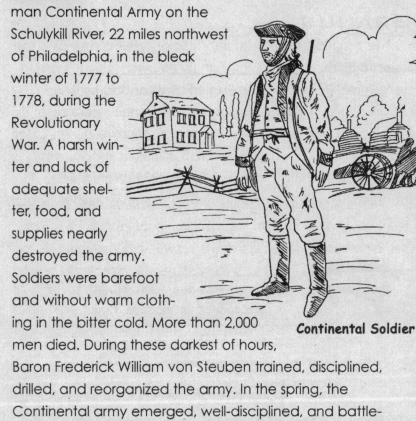

Continental Soldier

Vandals

Wherever the Vandals went in the early Middle Ages, they looted churches and wrecked cities and towns. A Germanic tribe originally from the banks of the Baltic Sea, the Vandals stormed through Gaul, Spain, and North Africa.

Their navy ruled the western Mediterranean. They plundered Rome in 455. Finally, in 534, they were subdued by the great Byzantine general Belisarius, and they disappeared from history.

FAST FACT

The part of Spain ruled by the Vandals was called Vandalusia. Eventually, the name became Andalusia.

Venus

Venus is the planet second from the sun in our solar system. It is slightly smaller than Earth. Thick clouds of water vapor and sulfuric acid shroud it, sweeping across the planet every four days. Its atmosphere is almost entirely made of carbon dioxide. Its surface temperature is 900° Fahrenheit, the hottest in the solar system.

Strangers in Our Midst

Which one does not belong? Solution, see page 143.

1. *a)* Valley Forge *b)* Baron von Steuben *c)* General Washington *d)* 7th Cavalry

2. *a)* solar system *b)* Venus *c)* USS *Enterprise d)* Earth

3. *a)* Belisarius *b)* Vandals *c)* Caesar *d)* Rome

vertebrates

Animals that have a backbone are called vertebrates. Vertebrates represent about 3 percent of all animals. There are 41,000 species of vertebrates. They include mammals, birds, reptiles, amphibians, and fish.

video games

Video games are games played using electronic devices and displayed on televisions, computers, or another type of viewing screen. Video games were first developed in the early 1970s.

Vikings

Otherwise known as Norsemen, these were seafaring pirates from Scandinavia (Norway, Sweden, and Denmark), who raided and plundered throughout Europe from the 9th to the 11th centuries. Excellent shipbuilders and navigators, they made long sea voyages. They created colonies in places as far apart as Ireland ("Dublin" is a Norse word) and Russia. Their settlement in France became

Viking

known as Normandy. The Norman invaders of England in 1066 were the descendants of Vikings.

FAST FACT

A video game called Pong was the first commercially successful arcade video game. It was introduced in 1972.

....

Subject Subtraction

Remove the first two letters from a word to make another word. Guess the first word, then remove the first two letters to get a second word, without rearranging any letters. Example: Remove the first two letters from a sea-faring pirate to get a monarch. Viking - king. Solution, see page 143.

1. Remove the first two letters from a guide to get an exit.
2. Remove the first two letters from a naval officer to get an indication.
3. Remove the first two letters from a hoard to get a tennis stroke.
4. Remove the first two letters from a club to get 2,000 pounds.
5. Remove the first two letters from a cost to get something cold.

vitamin

An organic compound that is essential in tiny quantities for proper nutrition, metabolism, and health. Vitamins help regulate certain bodily processes. They are in foods. The body is unable to make most vitamins, although some are sometimes produced within the body. Vitamin D, for instance, can be made in the skin when the skin is exposed to sunlight. Thirteen vitamins have been identified. They are A, eight complex B vitamins, C, D, E, and K. Certain substances, including choline and caritine, are vitamin-like but are made in sufficient quantities in the human body.

volcano

A vent or crack in the crust of the earth from which usually molten rock (magma), steam, and gas erupt as red-hot lava or violently explode into millions of tons of rock and ash. Earthquakes, vapor, lightning, and whirlwinds often accompany the explosions. "Volcano" also refers to the conical structure produced by accumulated eruptions. Volcanoes are classified as active, dormant, or extinct.

FAST FACT

Volcanic ash clouds sometimes are ejected high into the sky, posing a hazard to airplanes.

vulture

A large bird of prey related to the hawks, eagles, and falcons, but with weaker claws and a naked head and neck, living mostly on animal carrion (flesh from dead animals), but occasionally going after newborn or wounded animals. The California condor is one of the most endangered of all vultures. Its 10-foot wingspan makes it the largest of the flying birds of North America.

vulture

Building Words with Vitamins

How many words can you make from these essential vitamins: A, C, D, E, K, and B vitamins? Can you make more than 15? Solution, see page 143.

alnut

The walnut tree provides a beautiful furniture wood as well as the most important nut crop in the world. The tree itself is a favorite ornamental. The black walnut grows to 150 feet in height. The English walnut grows to 100 feet in height. Other members of the walnut family are the pecans, butternuts, and hickories.

walrus

Feeding almost exclusively on mollusks, the walrus is one of the most massive marine mammals. The walrus lives only in the Arctic regions of the Northern Hemisphere. A heavy and powerful animal, it can reach speeds of 22 miles per hour in the water. They will dive down to 300 feet to find shellfish. Walruses grow up to 12 feet long and 3,500 pounds in weight. Its upper canines extend into long tusks that may reach 3.5 feet in length. Walruses use their heads to break breathing holes in ice up to 8 inches thick. They use their tusks to widen the holes. The tusks are also used in fighting. Females give birth to a single calf and will nurse the baby for two years. Walruses can live for 40 years. Walruses have air sacs in their necks that enable them to keep their heads above water when they sleep. They molt, or shed their winter coat, every year in June and July.

Walruses are highly social creatures
and live in herds of several
thousand animals.

The Way of the Walrus

Wally the walrus has to make his way from the ice floe
to open water. He can't linger at Seal Central (too crowded)
or Polar Bear Boomtown (too dangerous). Can you give him a
hand? Draw a line showing Wally the best way to open
water. Solution, see page 144.

wampum

Polished shell beads were traditionally used as a currency by Native American tribes. They were also worn as decoration and insignia. The beads were cylindrical pieces of quahog clams or other shellfish. The beads were strung on strands of animal skin or woven into belts. Wampum belts were also used as a form of communication, their exchange confirming messages and treaties.

Washington, George

George Washington (1732–1799) was commander in chief of the Continental army in the Revolutionary War, chairman of the Constitutional Convention, and first president of the United States (1789—1797). Under great difficulties, he commanded the men who turned America from an English colony into a great nation. His ideals of liberty and democracy set a standard for his fellow Americans.

George Washington

water

Water is what we call the liquid state of the hydrogen-oxygen compound H_2O. Pure water is an odorless, tasteless liquid. It freezes at 0° Celsius (32° Fahrenheit) and its boiling point is 100° Celsius (212° Fahrenheit).

Water is the only substance found at ordinary tempera-tures as a solid, a liquid, and a gas. As a solid (ice), it is found as glaciers and ice caps, on lakes and ponds in win-ter, and as snow, hail, and frost. In the liquid state, it occurs as rain clouds formed of water droplets, and on vegetation as dew. It covers nearly three-quarters of Earth's surface.

FAST FACT

About 60 percent of the weight of the human body is water.

....

What's This Wet Word?

Can you figure out the "wet" word from the clue? Solution, see page 144.

Example: This 5-letter word starts with S and ends with M, and it is a form of water vapor. Answer: Steam

1. **This nine-letter word starts with H and ends with M, and it means precipitation of pieces of ice.**

2. **This eight-letter word starts with S and ends with L and it means a type of cold precipitation.**

3. **This eight-letter word starts with A and ends with S and means "water bearer" in astronomy.**

4. **This four-letter word starts with S and ends with M, and means "to move across a body of water."**

Weather

Weather is the momentary state of the atmosphere at any given time and place. The basic atmospheric conditions of weather include cloudiness, humidity, precipitation, pressure, temperature, and wind. These are organized into weather systems. Weather systems include areas of high and low pressure, monsoons, thunderstorms, and tornadoes.

whales

A whale is a large mammal that lives its entire life in the water. Whales have a fish-like body; however, their tail fins, called flukes, are horizontal rather than vertical, and they have paddle-like front limbs, called flippers. Their skin is smooth and glossy and, depending on the species, may be black, white, or a variety of colors and patterns. Beneath the skin is a thick layer of fat, called blubber, which provides insulation and serves as a source of stored energy.

Whales maintain a warm and constant body temperature of about 99° Fahrenheit and breathe air with lungs. They must come to the surface to breathe. Whales are enormous in size. The blue whale is one of the largest animals that has ever lived, reaching a length of more than 100 feet and a weight of 150 metric tons.

White House

The White House is the official home of the president of the United States. It is where the president lives and works. It has 132 rooms. The White House was first built in the 1790s, in Washington, D.C. However, during the War of 1812, it was burnt down by the British and had to be rebuilt. The White House was first officially known as the President's House and later, the Executive Mansion. It was not until 1901 when President Theodore Roosevelt made White House the building's official name.

FAST FACT

The White House has its very own bowling alley.

Organizing the White House

The White House has been rearranged. Put it back in order by writing the proper number next to the segment so that the building looks correct from left to right. Answer, page 144.

X ray

X rays are like light and radio waves. They are also a type of electromagnetic radiation. However, they can penetrate matter. Doctors are able to "read" X ray photographs and make medical diagnoses. They can detect foreign objects in the body, examine teeth for cavities, and study fractured bones. For specialized analysis of body structures, a form of X ray called CAT scanning is used. This process produces a three-dimensional X ray image. This makes it possible to see important body structures and soft tissues, especially in the brain.

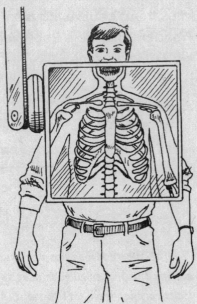
X ray machine

xylophone

This tuned percussion instrument is found throughout the world, in many cultures. It consists of a series of wooden bars of increasing length laid out in two rows. They are arranged like a piano keyboard. When they are struck with mallets, the bars will produce notes. Sometimes the xylophone can have bars made of metal or gourds beneath the bars to enhance the sound. Xylophones were developed and known in Southeast

Asia by the 14th century. In Africa, where the xylophone was possibly imported by way of Madagascar, its use spread throughout the continent, and the xylophone became a prominent instrument in African music. African slaves introduced the xylophone to Latin America, where it is known as a marimba. It arrived in Europe around 1500, and took root as a folk instrument in central Europe.

FAST FACT

Wilhelm Conrad Rontgen, a German scientist, discovered X rays in 1895.

Ex-rated Words

Some words have two different meanings, as do these words beginning with "ex." Can you identify these words from the clues? Solution, see page 144.

1. Which "ex" word means both to demand and be precise?

_____

2. Which "ex" word means both to exclude and only?

_____

3. Which "ex-" word means both tax and to remove?

_____

4. Which "ex-" word means both to put to death and to produce a work of art? _____

5. Which "ex-" word means to use up and engine gas?

_____

Yak

Related to the bison, the yak is a massive, shaggy ox used to carry and pull heavy loads on the high plateaus of Tibet. It has long hair that hangs down, touching the ground. Yak milk is rich and yields excellent butter and curd, and the flesh, eaten roasted or dried, is highly prized. The hair is spun into rope and woven into cloth, and the hide is used for leather.

Zebra

A black-and-white-striped member of the horse family. Zebras may be able to recognize other zebras by the pattern of stripes on their bodies.

Zebras are generally smaller than horses, with upright manes and shorter tails. Like horses, zebras have keen hearing. Zebras have chisel-shaped incisor teeth at the front of both jaws, and large molars, or cheek teeth, that grind up food before it is swallowed. A zebra bite is very dangerous because the zebra does not let go, but instead keeps grinding away.

zebra

ZOO

A zoo is a place where people keep and show animals, such as tigers, giraffes, and elephants, from all over the world. One of the earliest known zoos dates back to about 1500 BC, in Egypt. It was set up by Queen Hatshepsut.

FAST FACT

The Schönbrunn Zoo in Vienna, Austria, is the oldest zoo still in existence. It was opened in 1752.

Mixed-up Meanings

Take the letters of one word, reshuffle them, and you've got another word. Solution, see page 144.

1. Which mixed-up woman's name is a beast of burden?

_____

2. Which mixed-up way to solder is relative of the horse?

_____

3. Which mixed up resort is a snake?

_____

4. Which mixed-up pillow is a shellfish?

_____

Solutions

Page 3

able, Asia, bean, base, basil, blame, bomb, bone, lose, moan, nails, name, noon, now, owns, slow, women, won, wool

Page 5

1. chimpanzee ; 2. gibbon; 3. gorilla ; 4. orangutan;
5. monkey

Page 7

1. grizzly; 2. polar; 3. panda; 4. honey; 5. black; 6. bruin;
7. Malay; 8. hibernate

Page 9

1. honey; 2. sting; 3. queen; 4. hive; 5. bumble

Page 11

Camels # 1 and #3 are exactly alike.

Camel #2

Camels #1 and #3

Page 13

Page 15
"I think it's time we moved into the penthouse."

Page 17
1. Xanthosaur; 2. Dentosaur; 3. Sagittasaur;
4. Ophisaur; 5. Hydrosaur

Page 19
Who loves me will also love my dog.
1. heavy; 2. vowel; 3. gloom; 4. moos; 5. wild; 6. sell

Page 21
Pyramids A and D are exactly alike.

Page 23

1. elf; 2. elm; 3. elk; 4. elbow; 5. elevator;
6. Elizabeth; 7. Ellington; 8. elephant;
9. electron; 10. electric

Page 25

1. Adam's apple; 2. Benedict Arnold; 3. Braille;
4. Cadillac; 5. Edgar (Edgar Allan Poe); 6. John
Hancock; 7. Monrovia (James Monroe)

Page 27

1. Bering Strait; 2. Florida; 3. Greenland; 4. Pacific; 5. Mexico

Page 29

1. buzzard, 2. condor, 3. eagle, 4. falcon, 5. osprey, 6. owl

Page 31

1. rod > cod; 2. hike > pike; 3. shed > shad; 4. hole > sole; 5. tune > tuna; 6. puppy > guppy; 7. peach > perch;
8. spark > shark; 9. slate > skate

Page 33

Answers will vary.

Page 35

Numbers 1 and 4 are real galaxies.

Page 37

1. EMERALD
2. DIAMOND
3. SAPPHIRE
4. OPAL
5. RUBY
6. AMETHYST

Page 39
1. geyser advisor; 2. cheyenne cayenne; 3. custer cluster; 4. giraffe caraffe

Page 41
1. Whoopi Goldberg; 2. golden ager; 3. golden oldie; 4. golden retriever

Page 43

hail	hat
lane	lone
sail	sale
stone	tan
tin	toe
ton	tone

Page 45
1. tarragon; 2. dill 3. sage; 4. thyme; 5. bay

Page 47
1. bee; 2. blossom; 3. hive; 4. honey; 5. nectar

Page 49
1. Alice; 2. police; 3. apprentice; 4. choice; 5. practice

Page 51
1. bee; 2. beetle; 3. ant; 4. termite; 5. mosquito

Page 53

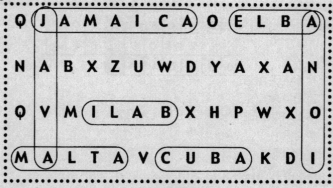

Page 55
4. Invented the lightning rod.

Page 57
1. jujitsu; 2. judge; 3. hand-to-hand; 4. bow;
Secret word. : J U D O

Page 59
Juggler number 3 is different from the others.

Page 61
1. Captain Kidd; 2. Jean Lafitte; 3. John Hawkins;
4. Francis Drake; 5. Henry Morgan

Page 63

1.	T	A	B	A	R	D
2.	H	O	R	S	E	
3.	S	Q	U	I	R	E
4.	S	I	R			
5.	K	I	N	G		
6.	L	A	N	C	E	
7.	A	R	M	O	R	
8. L	A	N	C	E	L	O T
9. M	O	U	N	T	E	D
10. H E	L	M	E	T		

Page 65
A. keg; B. tar; C. seal, GREAT LAKES

Page 67
a) gecko; b) monitor; c) iguana; d) chameleon

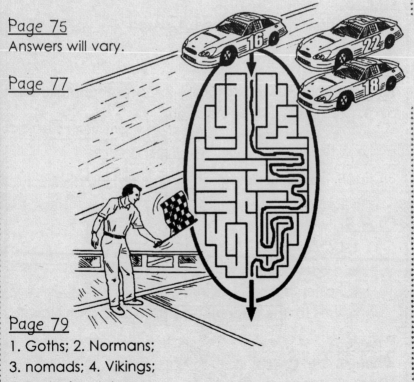

Page 69
Answers will vary.

Page 71
1. c) Bagdhad (Baghdad);
2. b) Lebenon (Lebanon);
3. a) Kerd (Kurd);
4. b) Shiek (Sheik)

Page 73
1. monkey; 2. ape; 3. gorilla

Page 75
Answers will vary.

Page 77

Page 79
1. Goths; 2. Normans;
3. nomads; 4. Vikings;
5. Bedouins; 6. Lapps.
Mystery Word: Travel

Act	Rot
Actor	Tar
Can	Tea
Cot	Ten
Ear	Tin
Ran	Ton

Page 83

TALL OAKS FROM LITTLE ACORNS GROW

Page 85

1. percussion; 2. listen; 3. reed; 4. organ

Page 87

1. All members of weasel family; 2. Gases that make up air; 3. Creatures that feed at night.

Page 89

cheetah, gorilla, giant panda, orangutan, tiger

Page 91

1. Lightning rod. Benjamin Franklin

2. Elevator. Elisha Otis

3. Pasteurization. Louis Pasteur

4. Uses for the peanut. George Washington Carver

Page 93

"Pigeon" stands for "head".

Page 97
1. Raining <u>cats and dogs</u>
2. Take a rain <u>check</u>
3. Come rain or <u>shine</u>
4. When it rains, it <u>pours</u>
5. <u>April</u> showers

Page 99
1. alligator; 2. crocodile; 3. lizard; 4. snake; 5. turtle;
6. python. Mystery word: anaconda

Page 101
1. Yazoo; 2. Hudson; 3. Wabash; 4. Swanee

Page 103
1. salary; 2. saline; 3. salami; 4. salsa; 5. salad

Page 105
WHITE HOUSE 1. hit 2. sue 3. Julia Ward Howe

Page 107
FEMUR
PATELLA
PELVIS
RIB
SKULL
TIBIA

Page 109
Winston Churchill

Page 111
Every tooth in a man's head is worth more than a diamond.

Page 113

Page 115

1. calm palm;
2. rare pear;
3. gaspin' aspen;
4. birch search

Page 117

1. astronomer
2. frozen
3. moons
4. orbit

Page 119

1. d; 2. c.; 3. c

Page 121

1. scout > out; 2. ensign > sign; 3. reserve > serve;
4. baton > ton; 5. price > ice

Page 123

ACE	BEAK
BACK	BECK
BACKED	CAB
BAD	CAD
BADE	CAKE
BAKE	CAKED
BAKED	DECK
BEAD	

Page 125

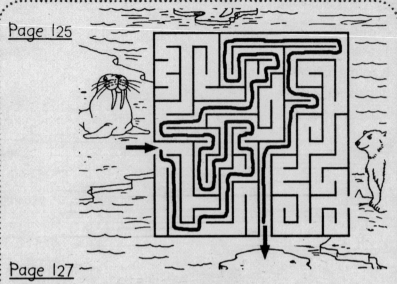

Page 127 ~

1. hailstorm; 2. snowfall; 3. aquarius; 4. swim

Page 129

Page 131

1. exact; 2. except.; 3. excise; 4. execute; 5. exhaust

Page 133

1. kay > yak; 2. braze > zebra; 3. spa > asp; 4. bolster > lobster